science for a changing world

The Regional Geochemistry of Soils and Willow in a Metamorphic Bedrock Terrain, Seward Peninsula, Alaska, 2005, and its Possible Relation to Moose

By L.P. Gough, P.J. Lamothe, R.F. Sanzolone, L.J. Drew, and J.A.K. Maier

Open-File Report 2009-1124

U.S. Department of the Interior
U.S. Geological Survey

U.S. Department of the Interior
KEN SALAZAR, Secretary

U.S. Geological Survey
Suzette M. Kimball, Acting Director

U.S. Geological Survey, Reston, Virginia: 2009

For product and ordering information:
World Wide Web: http://www.usgs.gov/pubprod
Telephone: 1-888-ASK-USGS

For more information on the USGS—the Federal source for science about the Earth,
its natural and living resources, natural hazards, and the environment:
World Wide Web: http://www.usgs.gov
Telephone: 1-888-ASK-USGS

Suggested citation:
Gough, L.P., Lamothe, P.J., Sanzolone, R.F., Drew, L.J., and Maier, J.A.K., 2009, The regional geochemistry of soils
and willow in a metamorphic bedrock terrain, Seward Peninsula, Alaska, 2005, and its possible relation to moose: U.S.
Geological Survey Open-File Report 2009-1124, 41 p.

Contents

Figures

Tables

Conversion Factors

Multiply	By	To obtain
	Length	
centimeter (cm)	0.3937	inch (in)
millimeter (mm)	0.03937	inch (in)
meter (m)	3.281	foot (ft)
kilometer (km)	0.6214	mile (mi)
	Area	
square meter (m^2)	0.0002471	acre
square kilometer (km^2)	0.3861	square mile (mi^2)

Temperature in degrees Celsius (°C) may be converted to degrees Fahrenheit (°F) as follows:
°F=(1.8×°C)+32

The Regional Geochemistry of Soils and Willow in a Metamorphic Bedrock Terrain, Seward Peninsula, Alaska, 2005, and its Possible Relation to Moose

By L.P. Gough,[1] P.J. Lamothe,[2] R.F. Sanzolone,[2] L.J. Drew,[1] and J.A.K. Maier[3]

Abstract

In 2005 willow leaves (all variants of *Salix pulchra*) and A-, B-, and C-horizon soils were sampled at 10 sites along a transect near the Quarry prospect and 11 sites along a transect near the Big Hurrah mine for the purpose of defining the spatial variability of elements and the regional geochemistry of willow and soil over Paleozoic metamorphic rocks potentially high in cadmium (Cd). Willow, a favorite browse of moose (*Alces alces*), has been shown by various investigators to bioaccumulate Cd. Moose in this region show clinical signs of tooth wear and breakage and are declining in population for unknown reasons. A trace element imbalance in their diet has been proposed as a possible cause for these observations. Cadmium, in high enough concentrations, is one dietary trace element that potentially could produce such symptoms.

We report both the summary statistics for elements in willow and soils and the results of an unbalanced, one-way, hierarchical analysis of variance (ANOVA) (general linear model, GLM), which was constructed to measure the geochemical variability in willow (and soil) at various distance scales across the Paleozoic geologic unit high in bioavailable Cd. All of the geochemical data are presented in the Appendices. The two locations are separated by approximately 80 kilometers (km); sites within a location are approximately 0.5 kilometers apart. Duplicate samples collected within a site were separated by 0.05 km or slightly less. Results of the GLM are element specific and range from having very little regional variability to having most of their variance at the top (greater than 80 km) level. For willow, a significant proportion of the total variance occurred at the "between locations" level for ash yield, barium (Ba), Cd, calcium (Ca), cobalt (Co), nickel (Ni), and zinc (Zn). For soils, concentrations of elements in all three soil horizons were similar in that most of the variability in the geochemical data occurred at the "between locations" and the "among sites at a location" GLM levels.

Most of the variation in concentrations of Cd in soils occurred among sites (separated by 0.5 km) at both locations across all soil horizons and not between the two locations. Cd distribution across the landscape may be due to variation in soil mineralogy, especially the amount of graphite in soil, which has been associated with Cd. Although samples were collected on the same geologic unit, the geochemistry of soils was demonstrated to be uniform with depth but highly variable between locations separated by 80 km. This exploratory study establishes the presence of elevated levels of Cd in willow

---

[1] U.S. Geological Survey, Reston, VA.
[2] U.S. Geological Survey, Denver, CO.
[3] University of Alaska—Fairbanks, Fairbanks, AK.

growing over Paleozoic bedrock in the Seward Peninsula. Further work is needed to definitively link these high Cd levels in willow browse to the health of moose.

Introduction

In 2002 the U.S. Geological Survey (USGS) began looking at the relation between regional geology and the geochemistry of soils and vegetation that occur in specific geologic terrains. We were especially interested in how soil geochemistry and the uptake and bioaccumulation of toxic trace elements by native vegetation growing in those soils might ultimately affect the health of native animals such as moose (*Alces alces* L) (Brazil and Ferguson, 1989; Eisler, 1985; Gough and others, 2006). This relation becomes increasingly important if the animal's health is threatened (Glooschenko and others, 1988). Moose are an essential cultural and economic resource in northern regions and thus are a primary focus of resource management agencies (Maier and others, 2005). Therefore, the health and numbers of moose are critically studied (Schmidt and others, 2008). Accounts of moose tooth breakage and enamel defects in a declining moose population in the Seward Peninsula, Alaska, were of special interest (Smith, 1992; Rozell, 2003; Stimmelmayr and others, 2006). Tooth wear and breakage in moose harvested in the area of Nome, Alaska, were reported by Smith (1992), Rozell (2003), and Stimmelmayr and others (2006) to be greater than in moose harvested elsewhere in North America. Smith (1992) notes that all Seward Peninsula moose examined that were ≥ 7 years-of-age had broken incisiform teeth. All of these authors concluded, however, that the etiology of the observed enamel defects was unclear. We propose that one possible explanation is an excess of Cd in browse that is preferred by moose. Moose that feed on willow can be exposed to high total concentrations of Cd (Gough and others, 2002). In excess, Cd has numerous known adverse physiological effects on the mammalian body. It negatively affects tooth and bone construction and uterus and mammary gland development, causes general growth inhibition, and can result in renal tubular dysfunction (Larison and others, 2000). In this report, the focus is on the biogeochemistry of Cd, but data are presented for a large number of major and trace elements that are routinely analyzed.

Several years ago (Gough and others, 2002; 2006) we reported on the ability of willow in Alaska to bioaccumulate Cd in its tissues at levels several times greater than those in other native vegetation. This appears to be at least partially related to a commonly observed linear relation between Cd in plant material and Cd in soils (Kabata-Pendias and Pendias, 2001). However, willow will accumulate Cd in levels 10 to 100 times greater than levels in other plants (for example, grasses and grains; Larison and others, 2000; Gough and others, 2002). Kabata-Pendias and Pendias (2001) report that the Cd content of plant foodstuffs (grains, vegetables, fruits) ranges from 0.05 to 0.66 ppm (dry weight); whereas in this study we found willow to contain 0.65 to 42 ppm with a mean for the two areas studied of 3.0 and 15 ppm (tables 3 and 4). These levels are greater than those reported for willow in the Colorado ore belt (Larison and others, 2000). Cadmium uptake is affected by soil pH, soil carbonate content, and the soil clay content. Cadmium in plants is associated with its affinity for sulfhydryl groups and other side chains of proteins (Kabata-Pendias and Pendias, 2001). The affinity of Cd for proteins, therefore, is of particular importance to animals that feed on plants.

High levels of Cd in graze and browse plant species can cause health problems in some animals that feed on these plants (Eisler, 1985). For example, in a study of white-tailed ptarmigan in Colorado, Larison and others (2000) found that a winter diet of willow buds, which have a relatively high mean Cd concentration of 2.1 ppm (dry weight basis), resulted in renal tubular damage and increased chick mortality. Larison and others (2000) proposed that non-anthropogenic Cd, present in local soils formed over mineralized bedrock, was responsible for these localized abnormalities and might be a more widespread phenomenon than previously suspected. We hypothesize that Cd bioaccumulation by willow in areas in Alaska naturally high in Cd may be detrimental to the health of moose (Gough and others 2002) by being directly toxic (nephropathy; poor bone construction) and (or) by inducing Cu deficiency (Frank and others, 2000). In areas of Alaska (for example, the Seward Peninsula) that lack any other forage species, especially in winter, moose will consume willow almost exclusively and are known to have removed more than 55 percent of the current annual twig growth (Bowyer and Neville, 2003).

For the present study (2005) soil and willow (*Salix pulchra*) samples were collected at two locations—Quarry Prospect and Big Hurrah traverses—in the southern Seward Peninsula, Alaska, that are separated by about 80 km (figs. 1, 2 and 4). The purpose of the study was to characterize the scale of variability in the geochemistry of soil and willow in an area known to have both high Cd concentrations in bedrock and documented moose physical abnormalities. This assessment of geochemical variability would then allow others, more qualified in animal physiology, to make value judgments as to the importance of these data. The sites are situated within the immediate vicinity of abandoned mining prospects and (or) mines and are within geologic areas suspected to be high in Cd (John F. Slack, USGS, oral communication, 2004; Gough and others, 2008). At both locations samples of A-, B-, and C-horizon soil and willow leaves were collected and geochemically analyzed (table 1; Appendices *A* and *B*).

This report presents the results of analyses of soil and willow samples collected from 21 sites in two locations—Quarry Prospect and Big Hurrah traverses—in 2005. The samples were analyzed for 36 elements. However, our discussion focuses on the biogeochemistry of Cd. An analysis of variance (unbalanced general linear model) was used to determine the variability of concentrations of elements "between locations," "among sites at a location," and "between duplicate samples (both soil and willow) at a site."

Geology and Study Design

Location 1 (Quarry Prospect traverse), with 10 sampling sites, was located northeast of the Teller Road between the Sinuk and Cripple Rivers at approximately 64° 42' N latitude and 165° 45' W longitude (figs. 2 and 4). The area of Arctic tundra/shrub tundra has an elevation of about 230 m above sea level and extends from the Quarry Prospect (an excavated pit with abundant sulfide mineralization) northeast for 3 km. Sampling sites were placed 0.5 km apart with duplicate shrubs at a site separated by 50 m or slightly less. Bedrock geology of the area is composed of Paleozoic metamorphic rocks (Till and others, 1986; A. Till, USGS, written commun., 2009) and, based on the map by Bundtzen and others (1994), is within both the massive marble and the graphitic schist and quartzite members. Bundtzen and others (1994) describe the latter as either carbonaceous, fine-grained mudstones or mylonites. These units are known to be potentially high in Cd. The area has a long history of placer gold mining (Collier and others, 1908).

Location 2 (Big Hurrah traverse), with 11 sites, is east of the Council Road. The area of Arctic tundra/shrub tundra has an elevation of approximately120 to150 m above sea level (about 100 m above Big Hurrah Creek) (figs. 3, 5, and 6). The sampling traverse circumnavigates a low hill (identified on the C-5 quadrangle map as hill 596, its elevation in feet) and is in the southern half of section 33 at approximately 64° 40' N latitude and 164° 15' W longitude. Bedrock geology of the area is defined as Ordovician to Precambrian graphitic schist and quartzite (on the north, west, and south sides of the hill) and Ordovician to Precambrian schist on the east side (fig. 5). Both units are part of the Mixed Unit as identified by Till and others (1986) and Werdon and others (2005a, b). Like location 1, these geologic units are known to be potentially high in Cd. The area has a long history of placer gold mining (Read and Meinert, 1986; Kaufman, 1986).

Methods of Sample Collection, Preparation, and Analysis

Plant sampling was limited to the leaf material of the ubiquitous willow of the region, *Salix pulchra* (tealeaf willow; figs. 4 and 7). Hultén (1968) points out that this species is quite common in areas throughout Alaska and Canada, occurring within forests, at tree line and above, and in Arctic tundra. Hultén makes note of the species' adaptability and propensity to form hybrids. In general, however, it is an easy willow species to identify in the field, even without the flower or seeds, because of its broad, diamond-shaped to elliptical leaves and its tendency to retain the previous year's leaves and stipules (small, sub-leaves). The latter trait makes the shrubs quite easy to identify at a distance. It is obvious from field observations of browsing patterns that moose browse on both leaf and twig material. The leaf material from at least three adjacent shrubs (in a radius of approximately 5 m from a soil pit) was composited, put into cloth sample bags, and allowed to air dry.

In general, soils of the Seward Peninsula ecoregion (Nowacki and others, 2002) are sometimes referred to as the Norton Sound Highlands (Rieger and others, 1979) and are classified as Pergelic Cryaquepts to Pergelic Cryorthents (Rieger and others, 1979). These soils belong to the Soil Order Inceptisol, are both poorly and well drained, are underlain by permafrost, and are commonly formed in gravelly colluvium. Permafrost is pervasive but depth to permafrost is variable depending on aspect and elevation. Soil sample pits were dug to a depth that included the C horizon. Pit depth was determined by the presence of permafrost and (or) bedrock; however, C-horizon material was collected at each site. Soil pits varied in depth from 15 to 90 cm. Every sample collected was a mixture of soil that originated from the weathering of, most commonly, colluvial bedrock and loess. A-, B-, and C-horizon materials were collected, rocks were removed, and approximately 0.5 kg of the material was put into paper soil sample bags.

In the laboratory, willow leaf material was removed from the cloth sampling bags, placed in Teflon® beakers, submerged and rinsed in deionized water, and drained. This process was repeated three times. The material was then placed in plastic colanders, rinsed briefly with deionized water, and allowed to drip drain. Colanders then were placed directly into ovens, and the material was dried, using forced air at ambient room temperature, for several days until completely dry. Samples then were milled in a Wiley® mill to pass through a 2-mm sieve. Splits of the milled plant material were ashed in an oven at 450 to 500° C for 18 hours, and the ash yield was determined.

Soil samples were dried under forced air at ambient temperature. The air-dried samples were disaggregated in a mechanical mortar and pestle and sieved at 2 mm (10 mesh), and the minus-2-mm fraction was saved for further analysis. A split of the minus-2-mm material was ground to pass through a 0.15-mm sieve, using an agate shatter box, and this material was used for chemical analysis.

Soil and plant-ash samples were analyzed for 36 elements, using inductively coupled plasma-mass spectrometry (ICP-MS, table 1). In addition, the concentration of F, in the dry material of both soils and plants, was determined using ion-selective electrode (table 1). The dry, un-ashed material was used in the determination of Hg with cold vapor-atomic absorption spectroscopy (CVAA) and ash yield with gravimetric analysis (GRAV) (table 1). The results of the analyses for all sampled material are presented in Appendices *A* and *B*.

Statistical Methods

The study design was constructed to measure the variability in the willow (and soil) geochemistry at various distance scales. An unbalanced, one-way, hierarchical ANOVA (general linear model, GLM) was performed (using SYSTAT 11, SYSTAT® Software, Inc.) to assess this variability. The two locations are separated by approximately 80 km. Sites within a location are approximately 0.5

km apart, and duplicate soil samples from within a site were separated by 0.05 km or slightly less. The analyses were performed on the log-transformed data (Miesch, 1976).

This statistical design allows the partitioning of the total measured natural variation into its component parts. For soils and willow, the first of three components (GLM levels) is related to differences between the two locations (Quarry Prospect and Big Hurrah areas). The second component is related to variability among the sampling sites within a location, and the third component is related to variability between duplicate samples at a site. The total $\log_{10}$ variance results column, in the GLM tables 2, 5, 6, and 7, is the sum of the variances for each level of the design (levels 1-3 plus the residual or error). Because nearly all of the 36 variables reported in these tables were used in the GLM analyses, it is reasonable to assume that some of these observations are correlated, and therefore, the significant results also are correlated. This implies that the level of statistical significance is not 5 percent but some larger, not easily determined, value. Nevertheless, we present the results of our GLM test at the 5 percent significance level; however, one should keep this caveat in mind when reading tables 2, 5, 6, and 7.

Any systematic error that might occur in either sampling or analysis was converted to random error by analyzing all samples in the laboratory in a randomized sequence. The GLM statistical analysis requires completely numeric data sets; therefore, statistics for elements that had reported values below the analytical limit of determination are not given (see GLM tables 2, 5, 6, and 7).

Results of Willow Analyses and GLM

Results of a one-way, unbalanced, hierarchical GLM for the biogeochemistry of willow leaf tissue, collected at the two locations approximately 80 km apart, are given in table 2.

Very little of the total variability in the element data occurred at the "between duplicate willow shrubs at a site" level (table 2). This means that willow shrubs separated by about 0.05 km or slightly less were biogeochemically very similar. For most elements, most of the variability (except for Ni, with a non-significant proportion) occurred at the "among sites at a location" level. Furthermore, a large proportion of the variance was not explained by the model and occurs as "residual" variance. For ash yield, and concentrations of Ba, Cd, Ca, Co, Ni, and Zn, however, a significant proportion of the total variance occurred at the "between locations" level. This means that, at least for these six elements and ash yield, the two areas are biogeochemically distinct even though geologically they are similar (both areas being underlain by graphitic schists and quartzite members of the Mixed Unit).

The willow data at the two locations (Quarry Prospect and Big Hurrah) were separated, and summary statistics were calculated for each location (tables 3 and 4, respectively). Only elements with complete data sets (no qualified values) were used in the calculations. Of the elements with an important (perhaps significant) proportion of variability occurring between locations (Ba, Ca, Cd, Co, Ni, and Zn), concentrations of four (Ba, Cd, Co and Ni) were significantly lower in the Quarry Prospect samples than Big Hurrah samples, and concentrations of two (Ca and Zn) were higher. The presence of the massive marble unit in location 2 may explain the Ba and Ca differences, whereas differences in transition metals Cd, Co, Ni, and Zn may be explained by variability in the amounts of graphite. For these elements, the geochemistry of the bedrock appears to affect the biogeochemistry of the willow.

Results of Soil Analyses and GLM

Results of a one-way, unbalanced, hierarchical GLM for the geochemistry of A-, B-, and C-horizon soils, collected at the two locations approximately 80 km apart, are given in tables 5, 6, and 7, respectively.

5

All three soil horizons are similar in that most of the variability in the geochemical data occurred at both the "between locations" and the "among sites at a location" GLM levels (tables 5, 6, and 7). The percent of total variance occurring at the "between duplicate soil pits at a site" level was uniformly very low (commonly <1 percent). The uniformity in soil geochemistry with depth (among the soil horizons) was strikingly similar. Concentrations of As, Ba, Ca, Ce, Cs, Cr, Cu, F, La, Mn, Mo, Ni, Pb, Sb, Sr, U, V, and Y differed significantly between locations 1 and 2 (80 km apart) across all soil horizons. The largest proportion of the variance for these elements occurred on a regional scale as part of the Nome Complex DOx geologic package (fig. 1). Most of the geochemical variation for Al, Bi, Cd, Co, Ga, Fe, Li, Mg, Hg, K, Rb, Sc, and Na, however, occurred among sites (separated by 0.5 km) at each location across all soil horizons and not between the two locations. In other words, the variability in the concentration of these elements was greater among sites at a location than between the two broadly spaced locations. For a small number of elements (for example, P and Ti), most of the geochemical variability was not among the three distance increments but in residual variance (error).

The concentrations of Cd, Mo, and Ca in each sample, for each location, by soil profile (A, B, and C horizons), are shown in figure 8. The general similarity in the concentrations of Cd between the locations is apparent. The concentrations of Mo are much greater at Big Hurrah than at the Quarry Prospect, whereas the opposite is true for Ca.

Summary statistics for the concentrations of elements in the A-, B-, and C-horizon soils at the Quarry Prospect are given in tables 8, 9, and 10. These data can be compared with similar element statistics for the three soil horizons at the Big Hurrah traverse listed in tables 11, 12, and 13. For example, Cd concentrations among the horizons, between the two locations, have similar geometric means, whereas Mo and Ca concentrations do not (fig. 8). The data in these tables can be used as preliminary geochemical baseline values for the two locations.

Relation Between Plant and Soil Geochemistry and Importance to Moose

The uptake of Cd by willow often exceeds the uptake by other vascular and non-vascular plant species (Gough and others, 2002). The uptake of Cd by willow was investigated in a geologic terrain suspected to be high in total Cd. Although the soils sampled in the Seward Peninsula (mostly Pergelic Cryaquepts to Pergelic Cryorthents; Rieger and others, 1979) contained transported loess material, they are predominantly residual and composed of weathered metamorphic bedrock and loess. The mineralogical composition of selected soil samples is given in table 14.

Cadmium uptake by plants is affected by a number of physical and chemical soil features. In general, as soil pH decreases, Cd uptake increases (Hough and others, 2003). Cadmium uptake generally increases as the total amount in soil increases. Low microbial soil activity, as in these colder soils, enhances oxic soil conditions, which enhance Cd uptake. Cadmium uptake decreases as sorption of Cd in soil increases, and conditions that can enhance sorption include high soil organic matter, high cation exchange capacity (CEC), and high soil levels of clay and Fe and Mn oxides (Adriano, 1986). Certain micronutrient deficiencies in plants (specifically Zn deficiency) can increase Cd uptake. The presence of permafrost and low soil temperatures will decrease Cd uptake; however, an increase in soil salinity can increase uptake.

Moose that feed on willow can be exposed to high total concentrations of Cd. In excess, Cd has numerous known adverse physiological consequences on the mammalian body. It negatively affects tooth and bone construction and uterus and mammary gland development, causes general growth inhibition, and can result in nephropathy (renal tubular dysfunction; Larison and others, 2000).

Excess Cd also competes with Cu, Zn, and Ca for active sites on enzymes, phytochelatins, and cysteine-rich metal-binding proteins (metallothioneins). Cadmium-metallothioneins (Cd-MT) have been shown to account for 40 percent of the total Cd concentration in kidneys, whereas Cd-high molecular weight proteins account for 30 percent, and free Cd ions, 10 percent (Kabata-Pendias and Pendias, 2001).

Cooking moose meat for human consumption has been shown to decrease metallothioneins but not overall Cd levels. In one study, 20 percent of individuals in several Dene/Métis Canadian Arctic communities consumed caribou and (or) moose kidney/liver 1.5 times per week (Receviur and others, 1997). Further, the biological half-life of Cd in humans is long and is estimated to be 10 to 20 years (Lauwerys and Hoet, 2001).

Studies in Finland have documented the possible negative health effects of the consumption by hunters of moose heart, liver, and meat due to the presence of high levels of Cd in the moose tissues (Vahteristo and others, 2003). The study showed that heavy users of moose organs in their diets have a relatively narrow safety health margin. A study by Arnold and others (2006) concluded that subsistence hunters in Alaska, in general, are not at risk from the consumption of moose heart and liver. However, they emphasized the continued need for close biomonitoring studies, and their sampling did not include moose from the Seward Peninsula.

This study could be used as a basis for the determination of Cd (and other elements) in willow and soil and of their areal distribution. The study may be useful in predicting the levels of elements in grazing moose.

Summary and Conclusions

This exploratory study establishes the presence of elevated levels of bioavailable Cd in soils and willow growing over Paleozoic bedrock in the Seward Peninsula, Alaska. In order to assess the scale of the spatial variability in the concentration of Cd and other elements in soils and willow, these materials were sampled at two locations separated by 80 km, and the variability of concentrations was determined using a general linear model approach. The greatest differences in Cd concentrations in soils occurred among sites (separated by 0.5 km) at a location across all soil horizons and not between the two locations. For willow, a significant proportion of the total biogeochemical variability of Cd and a few other elements occurred among locations (separated by 80 km). When one examines the distribution of Cd across the landscape, these trends may be due to the variation in soil mineralogy, especially the amount of graphite, as graphite has been associated with Cd. This work indicates the need for further studies to definitively link these high Cd levels in willow browse to the health of moose.

Acknowledgments

The authors thank personnel of the Bering Straits Native Corporation, and especially Irene Anderson of the Land and Resources Department, for historical moose information and for allowing us access to native corporation lands. We thank John Odden, geologist for NovaGold Resources, Inc., for being very accommodating at the Big Hurrah mine. Thanks also go to Alison Till, geologist with the USGS in Anchorage, and the Alaska Division of Geological and Geophysical Surveys for providing the geologic base used in our figures.

References Cited

Adriano, D.C., 1986, Trace elements in the terrestrial environment: New York, Springer-Verlag, 533 p.

Arnold, S.M., Zarnke, R.L., Tracey, V.L., Chimonas, Marc-Andre, and Frank, Adrian, 2006, Public health evaluation of cadmium concentrations in liver and kidney of moose (*Alces alces*) from four areas of Alaska: Science of the Total Environment, v. 357, p. 103-111.

Bowyer, R.T. and Neville, J.T., 2003, Effects of browsing history by Alaskan moose on regrowth and quality of feltleaf willow: Alces, v. 39, p. 193-202.

Brazil, J. and Ferguson, S., 1989, Cadmium concentrations in Newfoundland moose: Alces, v. 25, p. 52-57.

Bundtzen, T.K., Reger, R.D., Laird, G.M., Pinney, D.S., Clautice, K.H., Liss, S.A., and Cruse, G.R., 1994, Preliminary geologic map of the Nome mining district: State of Alaska Division of Geology and Geophysical Surveys, Public-Data File 94-39, 21 p., 2 sheets, scale 1:63,360.

Collier, A.J., Hess, F.L., Smith, P.S., and Brooks, A.H., 1908, The gold placers of parts of Seward Peninsula, Alaska, including the Nome, Council, Kougarok, Port Clarence, and Goodhope precincts: U.S. Geological Survey Bulletin 328, 343 p., scale 1:250,000.

Crock, J.G., Arbogast, B.F., and Lamothe, P.J., 1999, Laboratory methods for the analysis of environmental samples, *in* Plumlee, G.S., and Logsdon, M.J., eds., Review in economic geology volume 6A, The environmental geochemistry of mineral deposits, Part A: Processes, techniques, and health issues: Society of Economic Geologists, p. 265-287.

Eisler, R., 1985, Cadmium hazards to fish, wildlife, and invertebrates—a synoptic review: U.S. Fish and Wildlife Service, Biology Report, v. 85, 46 p.

Frank, A., Danielsson, R. and Jones, B., 2000, The 'mysterious' disease in Swedish moose. Concentrations of trace elements in liver and kidneys and clinical chemistry. Comparison with experimental molybdenosis and copper deficiency in the goat: The Science of the Total Environment, v. 249, p. 107-122.

Glooschenko, V., Downes, C., Frank, R., Braun, H.E., Addison, E.M., and Hickie, J., 1988, Cadmium levels in Ontario moose and deer in relation to soil sensitivity to acid precipitation: Science of the Total Environment, v. 71, p. 173-186.

Gough, L.P., Crock, J.G., and Day, W.C., 2002, Cadmium accumulation in browse vegetation, Alaska— implication for animal health, *in* Skinner, H.C.W., and Berger, A., eds., Geology and Health—Closing the Gap: New York, Oxford University Press, p. 77-78.

Gough, L.P., Lamothe, P.J., Sanzolone, R.F., Crock, J.G., and Foster, A.L., 2006, Cadmium mobility and bioaccumulation by willow, *in* Winfree, R.A., Alaska Park Science—Crossing Boundaries in a Changing Environment: Proceedings of the Central Alaska Park Science Symposium, v. 6, p. 49-52.

Gough, L.P., Crock, J.G., Wang, B., Day, W.C., Eberl, D.D., Sanzolone, R.F., and Lamothe, P.J., 2008, Substrate geochemistry and soil development in boreal forest and tundra ecosystems in the Yukon-Tanana Upland and Seward Peninsula, Alaska: U.S. Geological Survey Scientific Investigations Report 2008-5010, 18 p.

Hough, R.L., Young, S.D., and Crout, N.M., 2003, Modeling of Cd, Cu, Ni, Pb and Zn uptake, by winter wheat and forage maize, from a sewage disposal farm: Soil Use and Management, v. 19, p. 19-27.

Hultén, Eric, 1968, Flora of Alaska and neighboring territories: Stanford, CA, Stanford University Press, 1008 p.

Kabata-Pendias, Alina, and Pendias, Henryk, 2001, Trace elements in soils and plants: Boca Raton, FL, CRC Press, 413 p.

Kaufman, D.S., 1986, Surficial geologic map of the Solomon, Bendeleben, and southern part of the Kotzebue quadrangles, western Alaska: U.S. Geological Survey Miscellaneous Field Studies Map MF01838-A, 1 sheet, scale 1:250,000.

Larison, J.R., Likens, G.E., Fitzpatrick, J.W., and Crock, J.G., 2000, Cadmium toxicity among wildlife in the Colorado Rocky Mountains: Nature, v. 406, p. 181-183.

Lauwerys, R.R., and Hoet, Perrine, 2001, Industrial chemical exposure: Guidelines for biological monitoring: Boca Raton, FL, CRC Press, 638 p.

Maier, J.A.K., Ver Hoef, J.M., McGuire, A.D., Bowyer, R.T., Saperstein, Lisa, and Maier, H.A., 2005, Distribution and density of moose in relation to landscape characteristics—effects of scale: Canadian Journal of Forestry Research, v. 35, p. 2233-2243.

Miesch, A.T., 1976, Geochemical survey of Missouri—methods of sampling, laboratory analysis, and statistical reduction of data: U.S. Geological Survey Professional Paper 954-A, 39 p.

Nowacki, Gregory, Page, Spencer, Fleming, Michael, Brock, T., and Jorgenson, M.T., 2002, Unified ecoregions of Alaska, 2001: U.S. Geological Survey Open-File Report 02-297, 1:4,000,000 scale map.

Read, J.J., and Meinert, L.D., 1986, Gold-bearing quartz vein mineralization at the Big Hurrah mine, Seward Peninsula, Alaska: Economic Geology, v. 81, p. 1,760-1,774.

Receviur, O., Boulay, M., and Kuhnlein, H.V., 1997, Decreasing traditional food use affects diet quality for adult Dene/Métis in 16 communities of the Canadian Northwest Territories: The Journal of Nutrition, v. 127, p. 2179-2186.

Rieger, Samuel, Schoephorster, D.B., and Furbush, C.E., 1979, Exploratory soil survey of Alaska: Washington, D.C., U.S. Department of Agriculture, Soil Conservation Service, 213 p.

Rozell, Ned, 2003, The mystery of the broken moose teeth: University of Alaska—Fairbanks, Alaska Science Forum Article 1669, accessed October 21, 2008, at http://www.gi.alaska.edu/ScienceForum/ASF16/1669.html

Schmidt, J.I., Hundertmark, K.J., Bowyer, R.T., and McCracken, K.G., 2008, Population structure and genetic diversity of moose in Alaska: Journal of Heredity Advance Access, doi:10.1093/jhered/esn076, p. 1-11.

Smith, T.E., 1992, Incidence of incisiform tooth breakage among moose from the Seward Peninsula, Alaska, USA: Alces Supplement 1, p. 207-212.

Stimmelmayr, Rafaela, Maier, J.A.K., Person, Kate, and Battig, J., 2006, Incisor tooth breakage, enamel defects, and periodontitis in a declining Alaskan moose population: Alces, v. 42, p. 65-74.

Taggart, J.E., ed., 2002, Analytical methods for chemical analysis of geologic and other materials, U.S. Geological Survey: U.S. Geological Survey Open-File Report 02-223, unpaginated (available at http://pubs.usgs.gov/of/2002/0fr-02-0223/).

Till, A.B., Dumoulin, J.A., Gamble, BM., Kaufman, D.S., and Carroll, P.I., 1986, Preliminary geologic map and fossil data, Solomon, Bendeleben, and southern Kotzebue Quadrangles, Seward Peninsula, Alaska: U.S. Geological Survey Open-File Report 86-276, 71 p., 3 sheets, scale 1:250,000.

Vahteristo, L., Lyytakäinen, T., Venäläinen, E.R., Eskola, M., Lindfors, E., Pohjanvirta, R., and Maijala R., 2003, Cadmium intake of moose hunters in Finland from consumption of moose meat, liver and kidney: Food Additives and Contaminants, v. 20, p. 453-463.

Werdon, M.B., Stevens, D.S.P., Newberry, R.J., Szumigala, D.J., Athey, J.E., and Hicks, S.A., 2005a, Explanatory booklet to accompany geologic, bedrock, and surficial maps of the Big Hurrah and Council areas, Seward Peninsula, Alaska: State of Alaska Division of Geological and Geophysical Surveys, Report of Investigations 2005-1, 24 p.

Werdon, M.B., Newberry, R.J., Szumigala, D.J., Athey, J.E., and Hicks, S.A., 2005b, Bedrock geologic map of the Big Hurrah area, northern half of the Solomon C-5 quadrangle, Seward Peninsula, Alaska: State of Alaska Division of Geological and Geophysical Surveys, Report of Investigations 2005-1b, 1 sheet, scale 1:50,000.

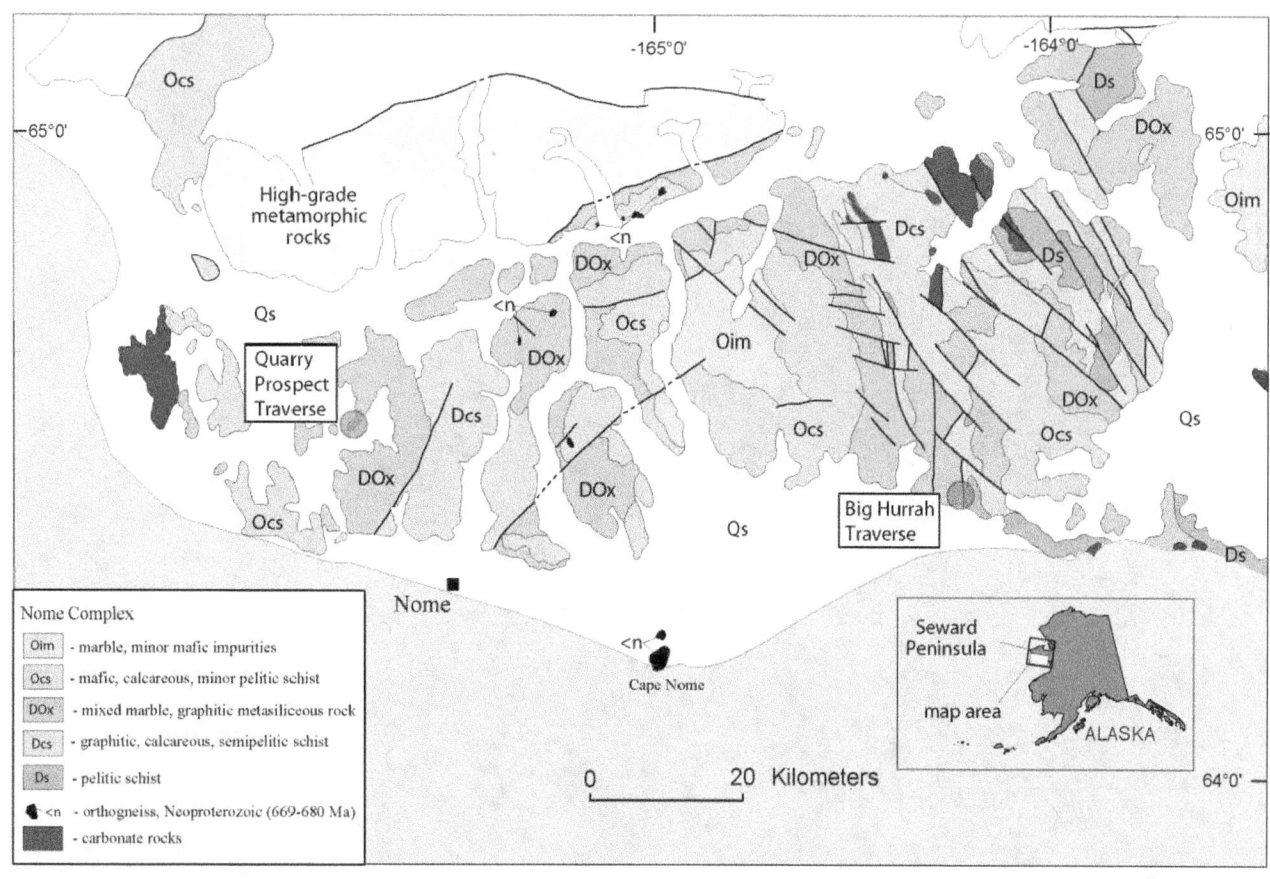

Figure 1. Base geology of the southern Seward Peninsula, Alaska, and the traverse locations. (Geology and base map courtesy of Alison B. Till, USGS, Anchorage, AK.)

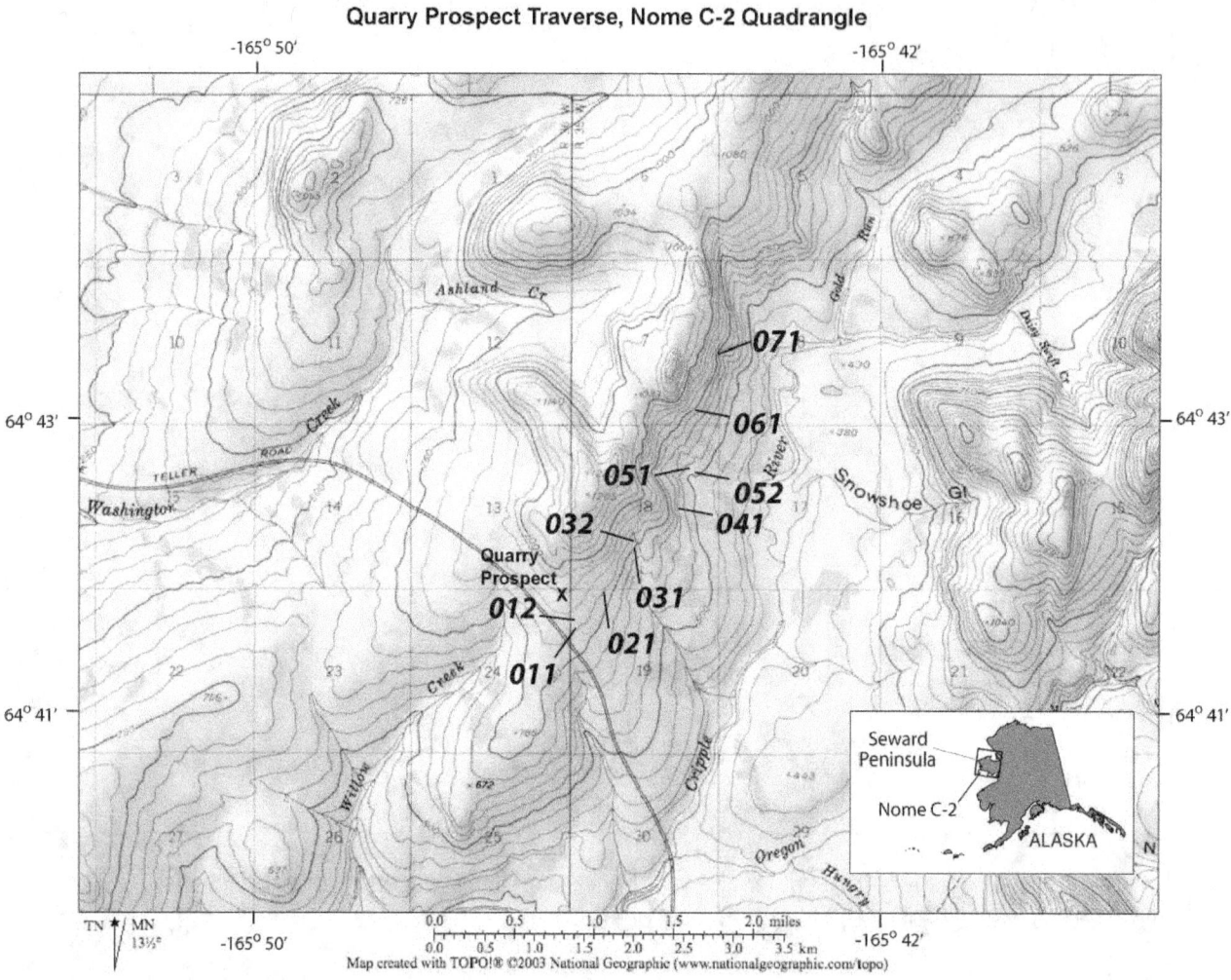

Figure 2. Location of sampling sites at the Quarry Prospect traverse off of the Teller Road, Seward Peninsula, Alaska. Sample site numbering corresponds to field number labels in Appendices *A* and *B* (for example, sample site 011 corresponds to sample 05AK011A).

Figure 3. View looking northeast below the Quarry Prospect traverse, Seward Peninsula, Alaska, showing the tall version of the common willow (*Salix pulchra*) found throughout the study area.

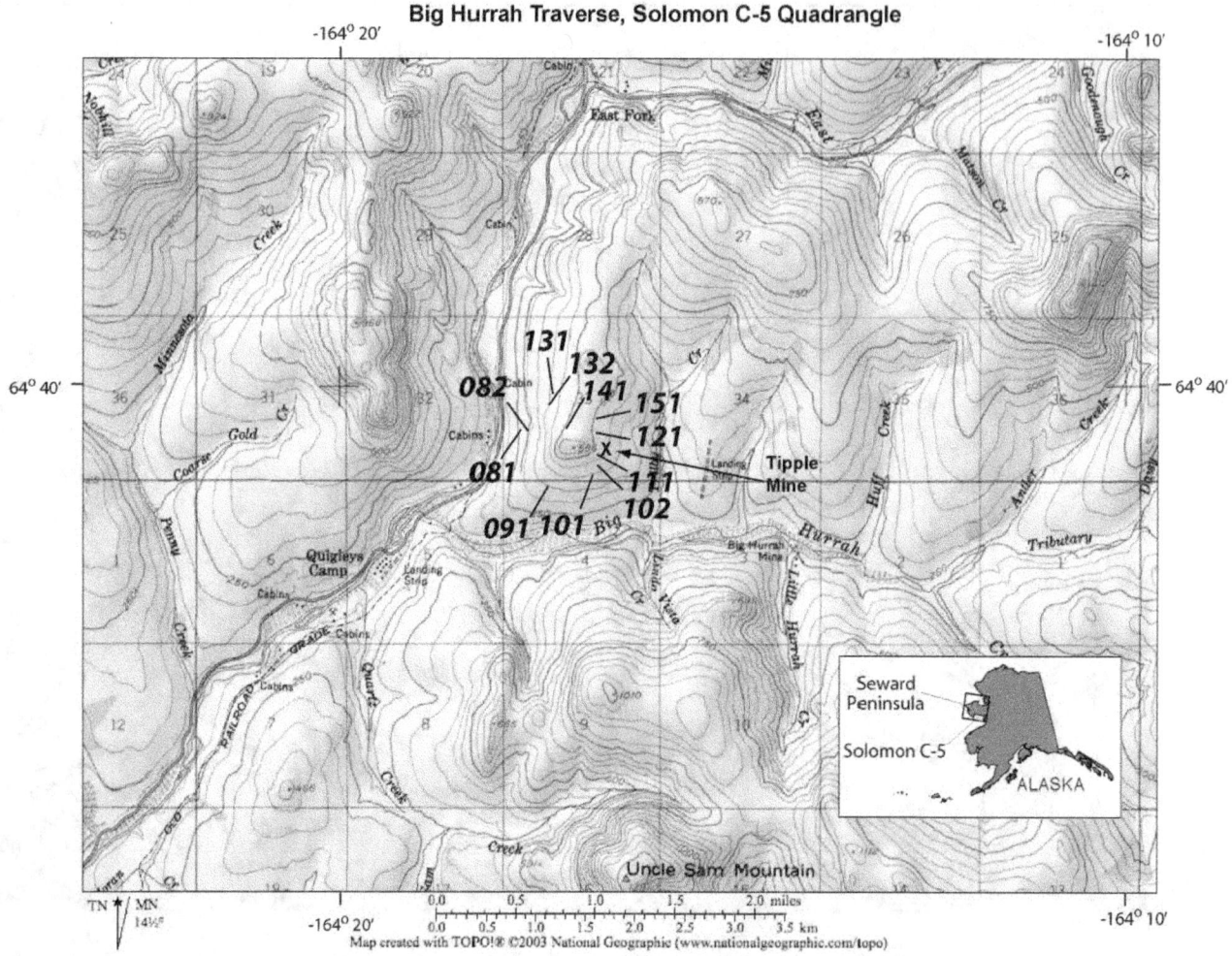

Figure 4. Location of sampling sites at the Big Hurrah traverse off of the Council Road, Seward Peninsula, Alaska. Sample site numbering corresponds to field number labels in Appendices *A* and *B* (for example, sample site 081 corresponds to sample 05AK081A).

Geology of the Big Hurrah Mine Area, Solomon C-5 Quadrangle, Seward Peninsula, Alaska

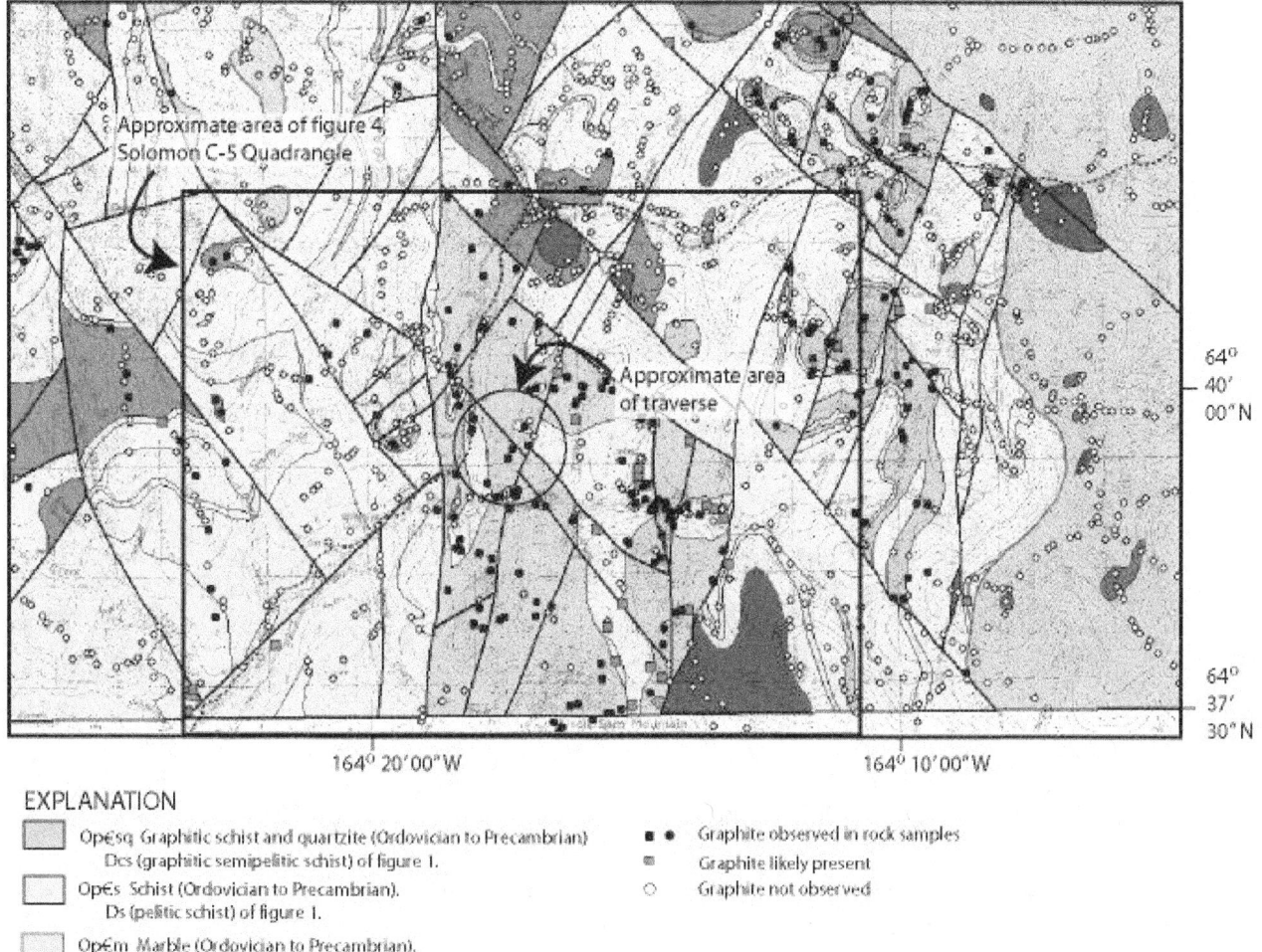

EXPLANATION

OpЄsq Graphitic schist and quartzite (Ordovician to Precambrian). Dcs (graphitic semipelitic schist) of figure 1.

OpЄs Schist (Ordovician to Precambrian). Ds (pelitic schist) of figure 1.

OpЄm Marble (Ordovician to Precambrian).

■ ● Graphite observed in rock samples
▨ Graphite likely present
○ Graphite not observed

Figure 5. Big Hurrah traverse location, Seward Peninsula, Alaska, superimposed over the regional geology (Werdon and others, 2005a, b). The geologic detail of the traverse area is emphasized. The presence/absence of graphite, observed in rock hand specimens by the Alaska Division of Geological and Geophysical Surveys, is noted (Melanie Werdon, written commun., 2008).

Figure 6. View looking southeast from near site 111, Big Hurrah traverse, Seward Peninsula, Alaska (see fig. 4). The structure in the foreground is part of the abandoned Tipple Mine, and off in the distance in the valley is the currently active Big Hurrah mine.

Figure 7. An area along the Big Hurrah traverse, Seward Peninsula, Alaska, showing the typical tundra vegetation with the abundant low-growing version of the common willow (*Salix pulchra*).

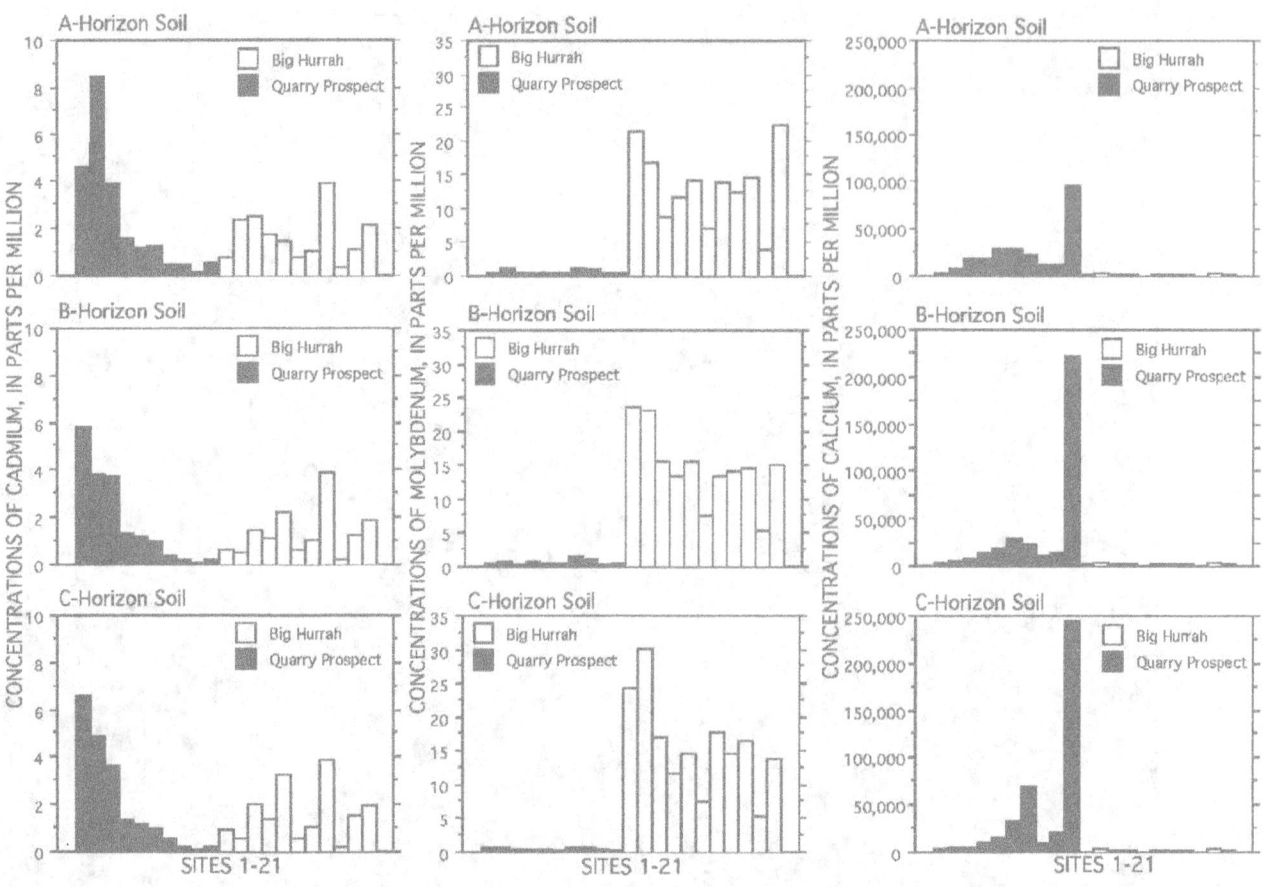

Figure 8. Concentrations of cadmium, molybdenum, and calcium in individual A-, B-, and C-horizon soil samples along the Quarry Prospect and Big Hurrah traverses, Seward Peninsula, Alaska.

Table 1. Analytical methodology used to determine constituent concentrations in willow leaf and soil samples.

[The methods follow those detailed in Crock and others (1999) and Taggart (2002)]

Constituent	Method of analysis
Concentrations of: Ag, Al, As, Ba, Be, Bi, Ca, Cd, Ce, Co, Cr, Cs, Cu, Fe, Ga, K, La, Li, Mg, Mn, Mo, Na, Nb, Ni, P, Pb, Rb, Sb, Sc, Sr, Th, Ti, Tl, U, V, Y, Zn	ICP-MS[1]
Concentrations of F	ISE[2]
Concentrations of Hg	CVAA[3]
Ash yield	GRAV[4]

[1]Inductively coupled plasma-mass spectrometry following a 4-acid digestion.

[2]Ion-selective electrode.

[3]Cold vapor-atomic absorption spectroscopy.

[4]Gravimetric analysis.

Table 2. Results of an unbalanced, one-way, hierarchical ANOVA (general linear model) for willow (*Salix pulchra*) leaf tissue between the Quarry Prospect and Big Hurrah regions, Seward Peninsula, Alaska (fig. 1; Appendix *A*).

[Locations are approximately 80 kilometers (km) apart; sites within a location are approximately 0.5 km apart; willow shrubs within a site are separated by 0.05 km or less; n = 21; *, significant at the 0.05 probability level; significance is only approximate (see "Statistical Methods" section), <, less than]

Constituent	Total $\log_{10}$ variance	Percent of total variance			
		Between locations	Among sites at a location	Between duplicate willow shrubs at a site	Residual (error)
Ash yield	0.464	47*	22	1	30
Aluminum	.768	1	48	5	46
Barium	4.383	49*	19	<1	32
Cadmium	5.833	45*	23	<1	32
Calcium	1.570	51*	16	<1	32
Cesium	1.651	3	50	6	41
Cobalt	6.488	61*	12	3	24
Copper	.403	12	29	5	54
Iron	.417	3	50	<1	47
Gallium	.214	<1	45	2	53
Magnesium	.470	<1	34	<1	66
Manganese	5.491	5	51	2	42
Molybdenum	2.760	7	45	2	46
Lanthanum	.692	<1	49	<1	50
Lithium	2.208	3	44	<1	53
Nickel	3.353	74*	18*	<1	8
Phosphorus	.381	<1	36	5	59
Rubidium	.906	10	46	4	40
Sodium	1.105	2	60	<1	38
Strontium	1.035	3	57	<1	40
Yttrium	1.157	2	26	<1	72
Zinc	.849	15*	46	1	38

Table 3. Summary statistics for the concentration of elements and ash yield in willow leaf tissue, Quarry Prospect traverse, Seward Peninsula, Alaska (see Appendix A).

[%, percent; ppm, parts per million; <, less than; --, not determined]

Constituent and unit	Minimum	Maximum	Geometric mean	Geometric deviation	Detection ratio[1]
Ash yield, %	4.8	13	8.8	1.438	10:10
Aluminum, ppm	50	160	71	1.379	10:10
Antimony, ppm	<0.04	0.04	--	--	1:10
Arsenic, ppm	<1	<1	--	--	0:10
Barium, ppm	2.9	73	11	2.973	10:10
Beryllium, ppm	< .03	< .03	--	--	0:10
Bismuth, ppm	< .06	< .06	--	--	0:10
Cadmium, ppm	.65	26	3.0	3.571	10:10
Calcium, %	.62	3.70	2.00	1.891	10:10
Cerium, ppm	< .1	.13	--	--	5:10
Cesium, ppm	.02	.16	0.07	2.033	10:10
Chromium, ppm	< .5	.79	--	--	1:10
Cobalt, ppm	.08	.96	.26	2.457	10:10
Copper, ppm	4.8	14	8.6	1.471	10:10
Fluorine, ppm	11	19	14	1.201	10:10
Gallium, ppm	.04	.09	.06	1.315	10:10
Iron, ppm	58	170	98	1.350	10:10
Lanthanum, ppm	< .05	.1	--	--	5:10
Lead, ppm	< .4	.53	--	--	2:10
Lithium, ppm	< .3	1.9	--	--	9:10
Magnesium, %	.136	.520	.300	1.606	10:10
Manganese, ppm	39	220	87	1.699	10:10
Mercury, ppm	< .02	< .02	--	--	0:10
Molybdenum, ppm	< .05	.20	--	--	6:10
Nickel, ppm	.5	2.5	1.2	1.690	10:10
Niobium, ppm	< .1	< .1	--	--	0:10
Phosphorus, %	.302	1.00	.550	1.499	10:10
Rubidium, ppm	10	51	23	1.771	10:10
Scandium, ppm	< .04	< .04	--	--	0:10
Sodium, ppm	110	740	310	1.787	10:10
Strontium, ppm	13	110	50	2.096	10:10
Titanium, ppm	<40	< 40	--	--	0:10
Uranium, ppm	< .02	< .02	--	--	0:10
Vanadium, ppm	< .2	.20	--	--	1:10
Yttrium, ppm	< .05	.13	--	--	4:10
Zinc, ppm	91	640	250	1.749	10:10

[1] Number of values above the detection limit to the total number of analyses.

Table 4. Summary statistics for the concentration of elements and ash yield in willow leaf tissue, Big Hurrah traverse, Seward Peninsula, Alaska (see Appendix *A*).

[%, percent; ppm, parts per million; <, less than; --, not determined]

Constituent and unit	Minimum	Maximum	Geometric mean	Geometric deviation	Detection ratio[1]
Ash yield, %	4.7	6.3	5.3	1.117	11:11
Aluminum, ppm	< 50	150	--	--	10:11
Antimony, ppm	<0.04	0.05	--	--	2:11
Arsenic, ppm	<1	1.7	--	--	1:11
Barium, ppm	25	99	47	1.424	11:11
Beryllium, ppm	< .03	< .03	--	--	0:11
Bismuth, ppm	< .06	< .06	--	--	0:11
Cadmium, ppm	6.5	42	15	1.701	11:11
Calcium, %	.533	1.10	0.744	1.223	11:11
Cerium, ppm	< .1	.13	--	--	5:11
Cesium, ppm	.04	.27	.083	1.840	11:11
Chromium, ppm	< .5	< .5	--	--	0:11
Cobalt, ppm	.50	7.1	2.3	2.160	11:11
Copper, ppm	4.6	11	6.7	1.258	11:11
Fluorine, ppm	9.0	16	12	1.219	11:11
Gallium, ppm	.04	.09	.06	1.241	11:11
Iron, ppm	59	200	100	1.442	11:11
Lanthanum, ppm	< .05	.08	--	--	7:11
Lead, ppm	< .4	< .4	--	--	0:11
Lithium, ppm	< .3	3.2	--	--	10:11
Magnesium, %	.210	0.420	.303	1.239	11:11
Manganese, ppm	< .7	490	--	--	9:11
Mercury, ppm	< .02	< .02	--	--	0:11
Molybdenum, ppm	< .05	.33	--	--	7:11
Nickel, ppm	3.0	13	6.5	1.584	11:11
Niobium, ppm	< .1	< .1	--	--	0:11
Phosphorus, %	.390	.780	.530	1.249	11:11
Rubidium, ppm	11	37	17	1.415	11:11
Scandium, ppm	< .04	< .04	--	--	0:11
Sodium, ppm	140	700	270	1.699	11:11
Strontium, ppm	25	63	41	1.251	11:11
Titanium, ppm	< 40	< 40	--	--	0:11
Uranium, ppm	< .02	< .02	--	--	0:11
Vanadium, ppm	< .2	.50	--	--	2:11
Yttrium, ppm	< .05	.21	--	--	6:11
Zinc, ppm	99	290	160	1.369	11:11

[1] Number of values above the detection limit to the total number of analyses.

Table 5. Results of an unbalanced, one-way, hierarchical ANOVA (general linear model) for A-horizon soils between the Quarry Prospect and Big Hurrah traverses, Seward Peninsula, Alaska (see Appendix *B*).

[Locations are approximately 80 kilometers (km) apart; sites within a location are approximately 0.5 km apart; soil samples within a site are separated by 0.05 km or slightly less; <, less than; n = 21; *, significant at the 0.05 probability level or greater; significance is only approximate (see "Statistical Methods" section)]

| Element | Total $\log_{10}$ variance | Percent of total variance: | | | |
		Between locations	Among sites at a location	Between duplicate soil pits at a site	Residual (error)
Aluminum	0.563	8	54	1	37
Antimony	2.802	62*	8	<1	30
Arsenic	3.484	49*	12	<1	39
Barium	2.403	57*	18	<1	24
Beryllium	.451	13	41	1	45
Bismuth	.403	<1	51	1	47
Calcium	7.756	77*	5	<1	18
Cadmium	3.520	<1	48	6	45
Cerium	.730	39*	37	1	23
Cesium	12.369	21*	30	1	48
Chromium	.729	20*	34	<1	46
Cobalt	1.423	16*	64*	<1	20
Copper	1.010	51*	24	<1	25
Fluorine	.912	33*	36	1	30
Gallium	.470	3	54	2	41
Iron	.711	1	64*	<1	34
Lanthanum	.627	43*	30	<1	27
Lead	5.603	20*	48	<1	32
Lithium	.656	<1	48	<1	51
Magnesium	.726	<1	70*	<1	29
Manganese	3.988	61*	19	<1	19
Mercury	1.279	4	63*	4	29
Molybdenum	9.474	93*	4	<1	3
Nickel	1.219	32*	30	<1	38
Niobium	.742	<1	30	<1	69
Phosphorus	.468	<1	48	<1	52
Potassium	.989	18*	52*	2	28
Rubidium	.851	13	53	2	32
Scandium	.461	11	51	<1	38
Sodium	.690	3	54	2	41
Strontium	1.126	32*	15	<1	53
Titanium	.454	4	33	<1	63
Uranium	1.845	70*	11	<1	19
Vanadium	2.029	84*	2	<1	14
Yttrium	1.519	65*	12	<1	22
Zinc	3.239	12	36	2	50

Table 6. Results of an unbalanced, one-way, hierarchical ANOVA (general linear model) for B-horizon soils between the Quarry Prospect and Big Hurrah traverses, Seward Peninsula, Alaska (see Appendix *B*).

[Locations are approximately 80 km apart; sites within a location are approximately 0.5 km apart; soil samples within a site are separated by 0.05 km or slightly less; <, less than; n = 21; *, significant at the 0.05 probability level or greater; significance is only approximate (see "Statistical Methods" section)]

| Element | Total log$_{10}$ variance | Percent of total variance: | | | |
		Between locations	Among sites at a location	Between duplicate soil pits at a site	Residual (error)
Aluminum	0.432	7*	83*	1	9
Antimony	3.737	67*	9	1	23
Arsenic	4.106	50*	7	<1	43
Barium	2.426	52*	20	<1	27
Beryllium	.256	16*	68*	<1	16
Bismuth	.290	3	78	<1	18
Calcium	8.953	64*	6	<1	29
Cadmium	5.049	<1	43	2	55
Cerium	.827	51*	36*	3	10
Cesium	4.976	16*	56*	<1	27
Chromium	.706	33*	43	<1	24
Cobalt	1.528	6	69*	<1	25
Copper	1.464	71*	16	<1	13
Fluorine	1.139	24*	55*	<1	21
Gallium	.373	5	79*	1	16
Iron	.646	<1	79*	<1	20
Lanthanum	.554	52*	36*	2	10
Lead	5.086	17*	53	<1	30
Lithium	.421	3	68	<1	28
Magnesium	.758	<1	70*	<1	30
Manganese	3.038	41*	30	<1	29
Mercury	2.727	9	55	8	37
Molybdenum	10.862	94*	2	<1	4
Nickel	1.385	39*	25	<1	35
Niobium	.690	<1	42	2	56
Phosphorus	.699	1	44	<1	55
Potassium	.957	19*	64*	<1	17
Rubidium	.840	13*	66*	<1	21
Scandium	.381	9*	74*	<1	17
Sodium	1.337	7	59	<1	33
Strontium	1.396	29*	18	<1	53
Titanium	.414	6	41	4	49
Uranium	2.205	79*	10	1	10
Vanadium	2.079	92*	2	<1	6
Yttrium	1.240	74*	15	<1	11
Zinc	3.679	4	43	2	51

Table 7. Results of an unbalanced, one-way, hierarchical ANOVA (general linear model) for C-horizon soils between the Quarry Prospect and Big Hurrah traverses, Seward Peninsula, Alaska (see Appendix *B*).

[Locations are approximately 80 kilometers (km) apart; sites within a location are approximately 0.5 km apart; soil samples within a site are separated by 0.05 km or slightly less; <, less than; n = 21; *, significant at the 0.05 probability level or greater; significance is only approximate (see "Statistical Methods" section)]

| Element | Total log$_{10}$ variance | Percent of total variance: | | | |
		Between location	Among sites at a location	Between duplicate soil pits at a site	Residual (error)
Aluminum	0.361	7*	82	<1	11
Antimony	3.734	68*	11	1	20
Arsenic	3.752	49*	10	<1	42
Barium	2.605	49*	20	1	30
Beryllium	.237	16*	67*	<1	17
Bismuth	.264	1	87*	<1	11
Calcium	10.129	62*	7	<1	31
Cadmium	4.937	<1	47	<1	52
Cerium	.815	45*	45*	<1	10
Cesium	4.650	13*	57*	<1	29
Chromium	.587	35*	51*	<1	13
Cobalt	1.069	5	74	<1	20
Copper	1.739	75*	9	1	15
Fluorine	.978	25*	56*	<1	19
Gallium	.359	5	77*	<1	18
Iron	.607	<1	87*	<1	13
Lanthanum	.535	41*	48*	<1	11
Lead	4.696	17*	50	<1	32
Lithium	.337	6	72*	<1	21
Magnesium	.799	<1	75*	<1	25
Manganese	2.860	53*	24	<1	23
Mercury	2.440	7	38	3	52
Molybdenum	11.071	95*	3	<1	2
Nickel	1.115	49*	24	<1	26
Niobium	.506	<1	38	12	50
Phosphorus	.641	2	42	<1	55
Potassium	.928	17*	64*	<1	19
Rubidium	.797	12*	67*	<1	21
Scandium	.337	7	71*	1	21
Sodium	1.216	9	53	<1	38
Strontium	1.470	25*	20	<1	55
Titanium	.382	5	38	19	38
Uranium	2.365	86*	7	1	6
Vanadium	2.123	91*	3	<1	6
Yttrium	1.152	74*	17*	<1	8
Zinc	3.609	3	43	1	53

Table 8.   Summary statistics for the concentration of elements in A-horizon soils, Quarry Prospect traverse, Seward Peninsula, Alaska.

[%, percent; ppm, parts per million; <, less than; --, not determined]

Element and unit	Minimum	Maximum	Geometric mean	Geometric deviation	Detection ratio[1]
Aluminum, %	2.92	8.43	5.35	1.485	10:10
Antimony, ppm	1.8	9.5	3.9	1.775	10:10
Arsenic, ppm	10	37	18	1.580	10:10
Barium, ppm	290	2,700	650	2.088	10:10
Beryllium, ppm	1.2	3.0	2.0	1.401	10:10
Bismuth, ppm	0.13	0.28	0.21	1.298	10:10
Cadmium, ppm	.13	8.6	1.2	3.515	10:10
Calcium, %	.402	9.49	1.78	2.303	10:10
Cerium, ppm	34	94	54	1.385	10:10
Cesium, ppm	.88	15	4.7	2.274	10:10
Chromium, ppm	30	96	54	1.471	10:10
Cobalt, ppm	6.2	15	11	1.366	10:10
Copper, ppm	16	31	22	1.257	10:10
Fluorine, ppm	410	1,760	820	1.704	10:10
Gallium, ppm	6.1	19	12	1.483	10:10
Iron, %	2.56	4.31	3.55	1.210	10:10
Lanthanum, ppm	17	37	25	1.313	10:10
Lead, ppm	8.9	670	41	4.741	10:10
Lithium, ppm	12	46	25	1.545	10:10
Magnesium, %	.427	.772	.606	1.241	10:10
Manganese, ppm	480	1,740	1,130	1.516	10:10
Mercury, ppm	.05	.52	.12	1.965	10:10
Molybdenum, ppm	.44	1.3	.62	1.486	10:10
Nickel, ppm	12	42	22	1.472	10:10
Niobium, ppm	<2	11	--	--	9:10
Phosphorus, %	.063	.177	.118	1.367	10:10
Potassium, %	.648	3.68	1.62	1.764	10:10
Rubidium, ppm	33	190	84	1.744	10:10
Scandium, ppm	7.2	17	12	1.349	10:10
Sodium, %	.243	.803	.392	1.452	10:10
Strontium, ppm	54	260	100	1.622	10:10
Titanium, %	.101	.356	.201	1.493	10:10
Uranium, ppm	.97	2.6	1.5	1.312	10:10
Vanadium, ppm	44	120	78	1.385	10:10
Yttrium, ppm	19	34	26	1.250	10:10
Zinc, ppm	71	2,710	280	3.441	10:10

[1] Number of values above the detection limit to the total number of analyses.

Table 9. Summary statistics for the concentration of elements in B-horizon soils, Quarry Prospect traverse, Seward Peninsula, Alaska.

[%, percent; ppm, parts per million; <, less than]

Element	Minimum	Maximum	Geometric mean	Geometric deviation	Detection ratio[1]
Aluminum, %	2.66	8.96	6.63	1.422	10:10
Antimony, ppm	1.8	12	4.0	1.869	10:10
Arsenic, ppm	9.0	41	21	1.645	10:10
Barium, ppm	260	4,300	820	2.162	10:10
Beryllium, ppm	1.2	4-Jan	2.4	1.331	10:10
Bismuth, ppm	0.11	0.27	0.21	1.289	10:10
Cadmium, ppm	0.06	5.9	0.80	4.493	10:10
Calcium, %	0.281	22.3	1.52	3.252	10:10
Cerium, ppm	37	130	75	1.415	10:10
Cesium, ppm	0.20	16	5.0	3.454	10:10
Chromium, ppm	26	96	59	1.543	10:10
Cobalt, ppm	5.8	17	12	1.400	10:10
Copper, ppm	14	37	22	1.365	10:10
Fluorine, ppm	230	1,880	910	1.947	10:10
Gallium, ppm	5.5	21	15	1.463	10:10
Iron, %	2.60	5.21	4.25	1.233	10:10
Lanthanum, ppm	19	47	33	1.306	10:10
Lead, ppm	9.3	770	44	4.739	10:10
Lithium, ppm	13	47	29	1.440	10:10
Magnesium, ppm	4,700	9,650	7,250	1.218	10:10
Manganese, ppm	570	1,630	1,020	1.555	10:10
Mercury, ppm	0.03	1.1	0.09	2.990	10:10
Molybdenum, ppm	0.36	1.5	0.55	1.599	10:10
Nickel, ppm	10	45	25	1.533	10:10
Niobium, ppm	3.2	16	6.0	1.783	10:10
Phosphorus, ppm	520	1,450	960	1.424	10:10
Potassium, %	0.541	3.92	1.97	1.801	10:10
Rubidium, ppm	28	200	97	1.815	10:10
Scandium, ppm	7.1	18	14	1.298	10:10
Sodium, ppm	2,760	17,000	5,250	1.705	10:10
Strontium, ppm	52	570	120	2.009	10:10
Titanium, ppm	1,340	4,940	2,540	1.555	10:10
Uranium, ppm	0.96	2.4	1.6	1.286	10:10
Vanadium, ppm	46	140	91	1.365	10:10
Yttrium, ppm	27	40	32	1.147	10:10
Zinc, ppm	48	3,560	270	4.001	10:10

[1] Number of values above the detection limit to the total number of analyses.

27

Table 10. Summary statistics for the concentration of elements in C-horizon soils, Quarry Prospect traverse, Seward Peninsula, Alaska.

[%, percent; ppm, parts per million; <, less than;]

Element	Minimum	Maximum	Geometric mean	Geometric deviation	Detection ratio[1]
Aluminum, %	2.62	9.25	6.59	1.423	10:10
Antimony, ppm	1.9	14	4.4	1.844	10:10
Arsenic, ppm	9.4	52	25	1.712	10:10
Barium, ppm	250	4,900	850	2.276	10:10
Beryllium, ppm	1.2	3.4	2.5	1.334	10:10
Bismuth, ppm	0.11	0.26	0.22	1.296	10:10
Cadmium, ppm	.09	6.6	0.89	4.340	10:10
Calcium, %	.349	24.4	1.64	3.746	10:10
Cerium, ppm	39	100	83	1.325	10:10
Cesium, ppm	.13	17	5.2	3.885	10:10
Chromium, ppm	27	110	65	1.426	10:10
Cobalt, ppm	6.4	20	15	1.396	10:10
Copper, ppm	15	31	23	1.273	10:10
Fluorine, ppm	260	2,040	960	1.838	10:10
Gallium, ppm	5.4	20	15	1.477	10:10
Iron, ppm	25,400	58,600	47,200	1.301	10:10
Lanthanum, ppm	19	43	34	1.261	10:10
Lead, ppm	7.3	830	45	4.583	10:10
Lithium, ppm	12	48	30	1.436	10:10
Magnesium, ppm	4,700	13,700	7,900	1.368	10:10
Manganese, ppm	670	1,980	1,360	1.359	10:10
Mercury, ppm	.03	1.1	.09	2.908	10:10
Molybdenum, ppm	.33	.82	.53	1.401	10:10
Nickel, ppm	17	49	29	1.400	10:10
Niobium, ppm	2.8	13	5.8	1.620	10:10
Phosphorus, ppm	610	1,330	900	1.294	10:10
Potassium, %	.525	4.12	1.97	1.818	10:10
Rubidium, ppm	27	210	100	1.796	10:10
Scandium, ppm	7.0	18	14	1.318	10:10
Sodium, ppm	2,820	9,420	5,160	1.538	10:10
Strontium, ppm	48	610	120	2.153	10:10
Titanium, ppm	1,280	5,390	2,530	1.588	10:10
Uranium, ppm	.94	2.1	1.6	1.264	10:10
Vanadium, ppm	44	140	94	1.389	10:10
Yttrium, ppm	30	37	34	1.076	10:10
Zinc, ppm	48	3,890	280	3.989	10:10

[1] Number of values above the detection limit to the total number of analyses.

Table 11. Summary statistics for the concentration of elements in A-horizon soils, Big Hurrah traverse, Seward Peninsula, Alaska.

[%, percent; ppm, parts per million; <, less than; --, not determined]

Element	Minimum	Maximum	Geometric mean	Geometric deviation	Detection ratio[1]
Aluminum, ppm	26,900	84,300	46,220	1.383	11:11
Antimony, ppm	6.5	35	15	1.752	11:11
Arsenic, ppm	24	210	77	2.363	11:11
Barium, ppm	1,230	3,060	2,280	1.302	11:11
Beryllium, ppm	1.0	2.7	1.7	1.346	11:11
Bismuth, ppm	0.11	0.35	0.21	1.493	11:11
Cadmium, ppm	.32	3.9	1.4	2.025	11:11
Calcium, ppm	640	3,740	1,480	1.793	11:11
Cerium, ppm	20	69	35	1.471	11:11
Cesium, ppm	< .003	6.2	--	--	10:11
Chromium, ppm	48	170	87	1.544	11:11
Cobalt, ppm	2.2	35	8.1	2.189	11:11
Copper, ppm	24	105	50	1.633	11:11
Fluorine, ppm	380	890	510	1.277	11:11
Gallium, ppm	6.8	18	12	1.331	11:11
Iron, %	1.11	10.1	3.64	1.835	11:11
Lanthanum, ppm	9.2	29	16	1.442	11:11
Lead, ppm	6.5	38	15	1.652	11:11
Lithium, ppm	12	47	27	1.529	11:11
Magnesium, ppm	2,900	21,200	6,400	1.827	11:11
Manganese, ppm	65	1,160	260	2.337	11:11
Mercury, ppm	.03	.17	.08	1.719	11:11
Molybdenum, ppm	3.9	22	12	1.634	11:11
Nickel, ppm	25	150	48	1.784	11:11
Phosphorus, ppm	490	2,110	1,120	1.514	11:11
Potassium, %	.596	2.37	1.11	1.303	11:11
Rubidium, ppm	36	110	63	1.326	11:11
Scandium, ppm	6.0	18	9.9	1.390	11:11
Sodium, ppm	1,830	7,210	3,510	1.538	11:11
Strontium, ppm	28	130	56	1.571	11:11
Titanium, ppm	970	2,820	1,820	1.384	11:11
Uranium, ppm	2.5	11	5.0	1.556	11:11
Vanadium, ppm	190	480	310	1.304	11:11
Yttrium, ppm	4.9	22	10	1.660	11:11
Zinc, ppm	86	280	150	1.514	11:11

[1] Number of values above the detection limit to the total number of analyses.

Table 12. Summary statistics for the concentration of elements in B-horizon soils, Big Hurrah traverse, Seward Peninsula, Alaska.

[%, percent; ppm, parts per million; <, less than]

Element	Minimum	Maximum	Geometric mean	Geometric deviation	Detection ratio[1]
Aluminum, %	2.79	9.20	5.61	1.333	11:11
Antimony, ppm	6.7	70	19	1.825	11:11
Arsenic, ppm	29	680	93	2.499	11:11
Barium, ppm	1,500	4,590	2,680	1.379	11:11
Beryllium, ppm	0.12	0.39	0.24	1.375	11:11
Cadmium, ppm	.2	3.9	1.0	2.332	11:11
Calcium, ppm	360	3,310	1,340	2.062	11:11
Cerium, ppm	20	69	41	1.351	11:11
Cesium, ppm	.2	7.2	2.2	2.695	11:11
Chromium, ppm	43	130	100	1.371	11:11
Cobalt, ppm	1.80	42	10	2.355	11:11
Copper, ppm	25	110	65	1.512	11:11
Fluorine, ppm	340	900	580	1.277	11:11
Gallium, ppm	8.1	20	14	1.246	11:11
Iron, %	1.17	11.0	4.71	1.781	11:11
Lanthanum, ppm	11	29	20	1.297	11:11
Lead, ppm	6.1	25	17	1.475	11:11
Lithium, ppm	19	47	33	1.377	11:11
Magnesium, ppm	2,670	23,200	7,760	1.879	11:11
Manganese, ppm	56	1,350	350	2.469	11:11
Mercury, ppm	.02	0.12	.05	1.878	11:11
Molybdenum, ppm	5.4	24	14	1.506	11:11
Nickel, ppm	24	130	61	1.744	11:11
Phosphorus, ppm	280	1,970	1,040	1.702	11:11
Potassium, %	.780	2.54	1.34	1.278	11:11
Rubidium, ppm	44	120	73	1.238	11:11
Scandium, ppm	5.6	21	12	1.387	11:11
Sodium, ppm	1,240	10,000	3,770	1.880	11:11
Strontium, ppm	32	82	60	1.344	11:11
Titanium, ppm	1,400	2,840	2,110	1.299	11:11
Uranium, ppm	3.3	15	6.3	1.489	11:11
Vanadium, ppm	320	450	380	1.131	11:11
Yttrium, ppm	5.0	23	12	1.490	11:11
Zinc, ppm	77	410	190	1.632	11:11

[1] Number of values above the detection limit to the total number of analyses.

Table 13. Summary statistics for the concentration of elements in C-horizon soils, Big Hurrah traverse, Seward Peninsula, Alaska.

[%, percent; ppm, parts per million; <, less than]

Element	Minimum	Maximum	Geometric mean	Geometric deviation	Detection ratio[1]
Aluminum, %	3.05	8.35	5.68	1.284	11:11
Antimony, ppm	6.5	78	21	1.852	11:11
Arsenic, ppm	34	610	99	2.407	11:11
Barium, ppm	1,520	5,020	2,760	1.415	11:11
Beryllium, ppm	1.4	2.7	2.1	1.183	11:11
Bismuth, ppm	0.11	0.36	0.24	1.357	11:11
Cadmium, ppm	.24	3.9	1.2	2.411	11:11
Calcium, ppm	270	3,460	1,260	2.075	11:11
Cerium, ppm	19	88	46	1.532	11:11
Cesium, ppm	.45	5.8	2.4	2.177	11:11
Chromium, ppm	47	140	110	1.385	11:11
Cobalt, ppm	2.5	36	13	2.042	11:11
Copper, ppm	35	140	76	1.582	11:11
Fluorine, ppm	340	900	610	1.294	11:11
Gallium, ppm	8.2	18	14	1.240	11:11
Iron, %	1.34	11.1	4.98	1.716	11:11
Lanthanum, ppm	9.6	36	22	1.434	11:11
Lead, ppm	7.6	28	18	1.432	11:11
Lithium, ppm	21	49	34	1.267	11:11
Magnesium, ppm	2,900	21,800	7,990	1.835	11:11
Manganese, ppm	65	1,310	400	2.324	11:11
Mercury, ppm	.03	.16	.05	1.687	11:11
Molybdenum, ppm	5.4	30	14	1.605	11:11
Nickel, ppm	33	120	68	1.599	11:11
Niobium, ppm	2.8	7.2	5.8	1.344	11:11
Phorphorus, ppm	290	2,300	1,040	1.732	11:11
Potassium, ppm	8,260	23,200	13,700	1.305	11:11
Rubidium, ppm	46	110	75	1.276	11:11
Scandium, ppm	6.0	19	12	1.378	11:11
Sodium, ppm	950	10,600	3,690	1.957	11:11
Strontium, ppm	36	88	63	1.264	11:11
Titanium, ppm	1,360	2,770	2,150	1.241	11:11
Uranium, ppm	4.1	12	6.7	1.448	11:11
Vanadium, ppm	320	480	390	1.142	11:11
Yttrium, ppm	6.3	25	13	1.510	11:11
Zinc, ppm	97	490	200	1.605	11:11

[1] Number of values above the detection limit to the total number of analyses.

Table 14. Site characteristics and bulk mineralogy (quantitative XRD) for samples of tundra soils developed from bedrock and loess, Seward Peninsula, Alaska, 2005. Data are from Gough and others, 2008. OpЄt, Precambrian mixed unit of the Nome Group (chlorite-rich schist and marble); OpЄsq, Ordovician to Precambrian mixed unit of the Nome Group (graphitic schist and quartzite).

[--, mineral was not observed; wt. %, weight percent; ID, sample identifier]

Sample ID	Soil horizon	Site elevation (meters)	Rock unit	Loss on ignition (wt. %)
05AK011A	A	248	OpЄt	8.8
05AK011B	B			3.5
05AK011C	C			4.2
05AK021A	A	233	OpЄt	41
05AK021B	B			3.5
05AK021C	C			3.5
05AK131A	A	128	OpЄsq	10
05AK131B	B			8.8
05AK131C	C			8.8

Weight percent

Sample ID	Quartz	Potassium feldspar	Plagioclase	Calcite	Dolomite	Amphibole	Pyrite	Goethite	Apatite	Rutile	Peat	Total non-clay	2:1 clay	Chlorite	Muscovite	Total clay
05AK011A	39	0.4	2.3	--	--	--	--	1.3	0.1	0.6	9.8	53	1.6	3.7	41	47
05AK011B	36	.8	1.5	--	0.1	--	--	2.3	.6	.5	3.5	45	2.2	5.3	48	55
05AK011C	35	.4	1.3	--	--	--	--	3.7	--	.7	5.1	47	2.7	2.4	49	54
05AK021A	19	1.1	1.6	--	.2	--	0.1	2.3	.2	.1	39	64	5.5	0.5	30	37
05AK021B	44	2.5	2.1	0.2	--	--	--	3.2	.3	.1	6.2	59	2.4	4.7	34	41
05AK021C	46	1.8	2.1	.2	--	--	--	3.7	.3	.1	6.5	61	3.0	4.0	32	39
05AK131A	45	1.6	2.1	--	--	--	--	2.4	--	.2	17	68	5.9	9.1	17	32
05AK131B	47	2.0	2.2	--	--	--	.1	2.3	.1	--	13	66	10	9.4	14	34
05AK131C	48	1.8	2.2	--	--	--	--	2.5	.2	--	12	67	6.5	13	15	34

Appendix A.

Concentrations of selected elements in willow leaf samples collected at selected sites, along with site descriptions and analytical methods, Quarry Prospect and Big Hurrah traverses, Seward Peninsula, Alaska, 2005.

[Samples were collected 6/12-15/05; ICP-MS, inductively coupled plasma-mass spectrometry; ISE, ion selective electrode; CVAA, cold vapor-atomic absorption spectroscopy; GRAV, gravimetric analysis; nr, not reported; %, percent; ppm, parts per million; <, less than]

Field no.	Laboratory job no.	Laboratory no.	Sample Description	Latitude	Longitude	Ash GRAV (%)	Ag ICP-MS (ppm)	Al ICP-MS (ppm)	As ICP-MS (ppm)	Ba ICP-MS (ppm)	Be ICP-MS (ppm)	Bi ICP-MS (ppm)	Ca ICP-MS (ppm)
Willow samples collected in the Nome C-2 quadrangle (Quarry Prospect) traverse													
05AK011SP	MRP-06835	C-274379	Salix pulchra leaves	64.69850	-165.76648	4.8	<2	71	<1	34.7	<0.03	<0.06	6,170
05AK012SP	MRP-06835	C-274380	Salix pulchra leaves	64.69863	-165.76579	4.9	<2	79	<1	72.9	<0.03	<0.06	6,660
05AK021SP	MRP-06835	C-274381	Salix pulchra leaves	64.70168	-165.75751	9.9	<2	61	<1	12.4	<0.03	<0.06	23,000
05AK031SP	MRP-06835	C-274382	Salix pulchra leaves	64.70548	-165.75104	7.6	<2	<50	<1	2.9	<0.03	<0.06	17,100
05AK032SP	MRP-06835	C-274383	Salix pulchra leaves	64.70580	-165.75117	12.8	<2	61	<1	5.0	<0.03	<0.06	28,800
05AK041SP	MRP-06835	C-274384	Salix pulchra leaves	64.70923	-165.74261	10.8	<2	<50	<1	3.9	<0.03	<0.06	30,300
05AK051SP	MRP-06835	C-274385	Salix pulchra leaves	64.71299	-165.74045	11.6	<2	76	<1	19.8	<0.03	<0.06	30,500
05AK052SP	MRP-06835	C-274386	Salix pulchra leaves	64.71261	-165.73900	11.1	<2	74	<1	19.4	<0.03	<0.06	29,400
05AK061SP	MRP-06835	C-274387	Salix pulchra leaves	64.71754	-165.73883	12.1	<2	156	<1	7.7	<0.03	<0.06	37,000
05AK071SP	MRP-06835	C-274388	Salix pulchra leaves	64.72247	-165.73430	7.7	<2	67	<1	3.2	<0.03	<0.06	18,300
Willow samples collected in the Solomon C-5 quadrangle (Big Hurrah) traverse													
05AK081SP	MRP-06835	C-274389	Salix pulchra leaves	64.66301	-164.29454	6.1	<2	132	<1	46.4	<0.03	<0.06	11,000
05AK082SP	MRP-06835	C-274390	Salix pulchra leaves	64.66302	-164.29359	5.1	<2	78	<1	24.8	<0.03	<0.06	7,980
05AK091SP	MRP-06835	C-274391	Salix pulchra leaves	64.65839	-164.28967	5.0	<2	<50	<1	52.3	<0.03	<0.06	8,430
05AK101SP	MRP-06835	C-274392	Salix pulchra leaves	64.66301	-164.29454	5.0	<2	54	<1	39.4	<0.03	<0.06	6,590
05AK102SP	MRP-06835	C-274393	Salix pulchra leaves	64.65976	-164.27770	6.1	<2	<50	<1	33.5	<0.03	<0.06	7,530
05AK111SP	MRP-06835	C-274394	Salix pulchra leaves	64.66183	-164.27782	6.3	<2	109	<1	41.3	<0.03	<0.06	7,230
05AK121SP	MRP-06835	C-274395	Salix pulchra leaves	64.66342	-164.27788	5.2	<2	148	1.7	47.6	<0.03	<0.06	8,820
05AK131SP	MRP-06835	C-274396	Salix pulchra leaves	64.66610	-164.28725	4.7	<2	81	<1	61.4	<0.03	<0.06	5,330
05AK132SP	MRP-06835	C-274397	Salix pulchra leaves	64.66584	-164.28813	5.6	<2	58	<1	58.5	<0.03	<0.06	7,920
05AK141SP	MRP-06835	C-274398	Salix pulchra leaves	64.66360	-164.28433	5.2	<2	87	<1	98.6	<0.03	<0.06	5,780
05AK151SP	MRP-06835	C-274399	Salix pulchra leaves	64.66396	-164.27846	5.1	<2	79	<1	47.8	<0.03	<0.06	6,790

Field no.	Cd ICP-MS (ppm)	Ce ICP-MS (ppm)	Co ICP-MS (ppm)	Cr ICP-MS (ppm)	Cs ICP-MS (ppm)	Cu ICP-MS (ppm)	F ISE (ppm)	Fe ICP-MS (ppm)	Ga ICP-MS (ppm)	Hg CVAA (ppm)	K ICP-MS (ppm)	La ICP-MS (ppm)	Li ICP-MS (ppm)	Mg ICP-MS (ppm)	Mn ICP-MS (ppm)	Mo ICP-MS (ppm)	Na ICP-MS (ppm)
05AK011SP	23.30	0.10	0.54	0.79	0.16	5.8	17.0	95	0.05	<0.02	nr	0.05	1.8	1,410	151	0.20	231
05AK012SP	25.70	0.18	0.96	<0.5	0.04	4.8	19.0	73	0.05	<0.02	nr	0.12	<0.3	1,360	83	<0.05	107
05AK021SP	5.00	<0.1	0.09	<0.5	0.10	6.7	15.0	86	0.06	<0.02	nr	<0.05	0.5	3,160	111	0.05	257
05AK031SP	2.10	<0.1	0.08	<0.5	0.02	6.4	16.0	58	0.04	<0.02	nr	<0.05	0.4	2,140	42	0.10	328
05AK032SP	3.60	<0.1	0.13	<0.5	0.04	10.7	16.0	97	0.06	<0.02	nr	<0.05	0.6	3,610	72	0.20	548
05AK041SP	2.40	<0.1	0.15	<0.5	0.04	12.0	12.0	100	0.05	<0.02	nr	<0.05	1.9	3,820	39	0.08	178
05AK051SP	1.60	0.11	0.50	<0.5	0.15	13.6	12.0	125	0.09	<0.02	nr	0.10	0.8	5,230	94	<0.05	312
05AK052SP	1.50	0.11	0.48	<0.5	0.14	13.0	12.0	122	0.09	<0.02	nr	0.10	0.7	4,970	90	<0.05	278
05AK061SP	0.65	0.13	0.16	<0.5	0.06	11.9	15.0	173	0.08	<0.02	nr	0.07	1.2	3,650	80	<0.05	740
05AK071SP	0.71	<0.1	0.60	<0.5	0.10	6.9	11.0	95	0.06	<0.02	nr	<0.05	1.3	3,360	224	0.20	573
05AK081SP	17.40	0.13	0.85	<0.5	0.06	7.1	15.0	131	0.07	<0.02	nr	0.07	<0.3	4,180	77	0.20	176
05AK082SP	9.40	<0.1	2.50	<0.5	0.17	6.9	12.0	106	0.06	<0.02	nr	0.05	0.5	2,540	125	0.26	176
05AK091SP	21.50	<0.1	2.70	<0.5	0.08	6.1	15.0	91	0.05	<0.02	nr	<0.05	0.5	2,850	220	0.24	139
05AK101SP	13.00	<0.1	3.00	<0.5	0.06	5.4	10.0	77	0.06	<0.02	nr	0.07	1.4	3,520	401	0.20	451
05AK102SP	14.80	<0.1	1.60	<0.5	0.05	10.6	11.0	105	0.07	<0.02	nr	<0.05	2.6	3,390	325	0.33	396
05AK111SP	41.80	0.12	1.60	<0.5	0.04	6.9	12.0	198	0.09	<0.02	nr	0.07	3.2	3,230	488	0.10	523
05AK121SP	8.40	0.13	0.50	<0.5	0.11	4.6	16.0	192	0.07	<0.02	nr	0.07	1.0	2,220	195	<0.05	181
05AK131SP	14.50	<0.1	7.10	<0.5	0.04	8.0	12.0	91	0.06	<0.02	nr	<0.05	0.5	3,540	<0.7	<0.05	204
05AK132SP	24.60	<0.1	4.90	<0.5	0.27	7.2	11.0	100	0.06	<0.02	nr	<0.05	2.1	3,390	125	0.20	253
05AK141SP	20.80	0.11	4.30	<0.5	0.13	7.5	9.0	59	0.04	<0.02	nr	0.08	1.7	2,060	110	<0.05	698
05AK151SP	6.50	0.10	2.60	<0.5	0.08	5.2	9.0	84	0.05	<0.02	nr	0.07	1.0	3,080	<0.7	<0.05	242

34

Field no.	Nb ICP-MS (ppm)	Ni ICP-MS (ppm)	P ICP-MS (ppm)	Pb ICP-MS (ppm)	Rb ICP-MS (ppm)	Sb ICP-MS (ppm)	Sc ICP-MS (ppm)	Sr ICP-MS (ppm)	Th ICP-MS (ppm)	Ti ICP-MS (ppm)	Tl ICP-MS (ppm)	U ICP-MS (ppm)	V ICP-MS (ppm)	Y ICP-MS (ppm)	Zn ICP-MS (ppm)
05AK011SP	< 0.1	2.3	3,840	0.53	14	<0.04	< 0.04	13	< 0.1	< 40	<0.08	< 0.02	<0.2	< 0.05	302
05AK012SP	< 0.1	1.6	3,020	2.20	10	<0.04	< 0.04	15	< 0.1	< 40	<0.08	< 0.02	<0.2	0.13	636
05AK021SP	< 0.1	0.7	4,820	<0.4	19	<0.04	< 0.04	44	< 0.1	< 40	<0.08	< 0.02	<0.2	< 0.05	441
05AK031SP	< 0.1	0.5	3,280	<0.4	11	<0.04	< 0.04	52	< 0.1	< 40	<0.08	< 0.02	<0.2	< 0.05	146
05AK032SP	< 0.1	0.8	5,620	<0.4	19	<0.04	< 0.04	87	< 0.1	< 40	<0.08	< 0.02	<0.2	< 0.05	245
05AK041SP	< 0.1	0.9	5,950	<0.4	37	<0.04	< 0.04	53	< 0.1	< 40	<0.08	< 0.02	<0.2	< 0.05	317
05AK051SP	< 0.1	1.5	10,000	<0.4	40	<0.04	< 0.04	95	< 0.1	< 40	<0.08	< 0.02	<0.2	0.06	248
05AK052SP	< 0.1	1.5	9,520	<0.4	38	<0.04	< 0.04	93	< 0.1	< 40	<0.08	< 0.02	<0.2	0.11	235
05AK061SP	< 0.1	1.0	6,440	<0.4	24	0.04	< 0.04	107	< 0.1	< 40	<0.08	< 0.02	0.2	0.07	158
05AK071SP	< 0.1	2.5	6,230	<0.4	51	<0.04	< 0.04	47	< 0.1	< 40	<0.08	< 0.02	<0.2	< 0.05	91
05AK081SP	< 0.1	7.6	4,810	<0.4	17	<0.04	< 0.04	39	< 0.1	< 40	<0.08	< 0.02	<0.2	0.07	292
05AK082SP	< 0.1	7.4	5,320	<0.4	21	<0.04	< 0.04	25	< 0.1	< 40	<0.08	< 0.02	<0.2	< 0.05	147
05AK091SP	< 0.1	3.4	4,670	<0.4	13	<0.04	< 0.04	44	< 0.1	< 40	<0.08	< 0.02	<0.2	< 0.05	196
05AK101SP	< 0.1	6.0	6,210	<0.4	15	0.04	< 0.04	44	< 0.1	< 40	<0.08	< 0.02	<0.2	0.08	99
05AK102SP	< 0.1	3.0	7,800	<0.4	11	<0.04	< 0.04	42	< 0.1	< 40	<0.08	< 0.02	<0.2	< 0.05	102
05AK111SP	< 0.1	6.7	7,110	<0.4	14	0.05	< 0.04	63	< 0.1	< 40	<0.08	< 0.02	0.5	0.10	183
05AK121SP	< 0.1	4.1	3,890	<0.4	15	<0.04	< 0.04	37	< 0.1	< 40	<0.08	< 0.02	0.2	0.05	196
05AK131SP	< 0.1	12.7	5,570	<0.4	12	<0.04	< 0.04	44	< 0.1	< 40	<0.08	< 0.02	<0.2	< 0.05	142
05AK132SP	< 0.1	7.1	5,720	<0.4	37	<0.04	< 0.04	36	< 0.1	< 40	<0.08	< 0.02	<0.2	< 0.05	176
05AK141SP	< 0.1	11.4	4,030	<0.4	23	<0.04	< 0.04	49	< 0.1	< 40	<0.08	< 0.02	<0.2	0.21	199
05AK151SP	< 0.1	8.4	4,470	<0.4	20	<0.04	< 0.04	38	< 0.1	< 40	<0.08	< 0.02	<0.2	0.09	138

Appendix B.

Concentrations of selected elements in soil samples collected at selected sites, along with site descriptions and analytical methods, Quarry Prospect and Big Hurrah traverses, Seward Peninsula, Alaska, 2005.

[Samples were collected 6/12-15/05; ICP-MS, inductively coupled plasma-mass spectrometry; ISE, ion selective electrode; CVAA, cold vapor-atomic absorption spectroscopy; no., numbers; ppm, parts per million; <, less than]

Field no.	Laboratory job no.	Laboratory no.	Sample description	Site description	Latitude	Longitude	Ag ICP-MS (ppm)
				Soil samples collected in the Nome C-2 quadrangle (Quarry Prospect) traverse			
05AK011A	MRP-06121	C-257767	A-horizon soil	Seward; A-hor. soil; 1st location, 1st site on Quarry traverse	64.69850	-165.76648	<3
05AK011B	MRP-06121	C-257768	B-horizon soil	Seward; B-hor. soil; 1st location, 1st site on Quarry traverse	64.69850	-165.76648	<3
05AK011C	MRP-06121	C-257769	C-horizon soil	Seward; C-hor. soil; 1st location, 1st site on Quarry traverse	64.69850	-165.76648	<3
05AK012A	MRP-06121	C-257770	A-horizon soil	Seward; A-hor. soil; 1st location, 2nd site on Quarry traverse	64.69863	-165.76579	<3
05AK012B	MRP-06121	C-257771	B-horizon soil	Seward; B-hor. soil; 1st location, 2nd site on Quarry traverse	64.69863	-165.76579	<3
05AK012C	MRP-06121	C-257772	C-horizon soil	Seward; C-hor. soil; 1st location, 2nd site on Quarry traverse	64.69863	-165.76579	<3
05AK021A	MRP-06121	C-257773	A-horizon soil	Seward; A-hor. soil; 2nd location on Quarry traverse	64.70168	-165.75751	<3
05AK021B	MRP-06121	C-257774	B-horizon soil	Seward; B-hor. soil; 2nd location on Quarry traverse	64.70168	-165.75751	<3
05AK021C	MRP-06121	C-257775	C-horizon soil	Seward; C-hor. soil; 2nd location on Quarry traverse	64.70168	-165.75751	<3
05AK031A	MRP-06121	C-257776	A-horizon soil	Seward; A-hor. soil; 3rd location, 1st site on Quarry traverse	64.70548	-165.75104	<3
05AK031B	MRP-06121	C-257777	B-horizon soil	Seward; B-hor. soil; 3rd location, 1st site on Quarry traverse	64.70548	-165.75104	<3
05AK031C	MRP-06121	C-257778	C-horizon soil	Seward; C-hor. soil; 3rd location, 1st site on Quarry traverse	64.70548	-165.75104	<3
05AK032A	MRP-06121	C-257779	A-horizon soil	Seward; A-hor. soil; 3rd location, 2nd site on Quarry traverse	64.70580	-165.75117	<3
05AK032B	MRP-06121	C-257780	B-horizon soil	Seward; B-hor. soil; 3rd location, 2nd site on Quarry traverse	64.70580	-165.75117	<3
05AK032C	MRP-06121	C-257781	C-horizon soil	Seward; C-hor. soil; 3rd location, 2nd site on Quarry traverse	64.70580	-165.75117	<3
05AK041A	MRP-06121	C-257782	A-horizon soil	Seward; A-hor. soil; 4th location on Quarry traverse	64.70923	-165.74261	<3
05AK041B	MRP-06121	C-257783	B-horizon soil	Seward; B-hor. soil; 4th location on Quarry traverse	64.70923	-165.74261	<3
05AK041C	MRP-06121	C-257784	C-horizon soil	Seward; C-hor. soil; 4th location on Quarry traverse	64.70923	-165.74261	<3
05AK051A	MRP-06121	C-257785	A-horizon soil	Seward; A-hor. soil; 5th location, 1st site on Quarry traverse	64.71299	-165.74045	<3
05AK051B	MRP-06121	C-257786	B-horizon soil	Seward; B-hor. soil; 5th location, 1st site on Quarry traverse	64.71299	-165.74045	<3
05AK051C	MRP-06121	C-257787	C-horizon soil	Seward; C-hor. soil; 5th location, 1st site on Quarry traverse	64.71299	-165.74045	<3
05AK052A	MRP-06121	C-257788	A-horizon soil	Seward; A-hor. soil; 5thlocation, 2nd site on Quarry traverse	64.71261	-165.73900	<3
05AK052B	MRP-06121	C-257789	B-horizon soil	Seward; B-hor. soil; 5th location, 2nd site on Quarry traverse	64.71261	-165.73900	<3
05AK052C	MRP-06121	C-257790	C-horizon soil	Seward; C-hor. soil; 5th location, 2nd site on Quarry traverse	64.71261	-165.73900	<3
05AK061A	MRP-06121	C-257791	A-horizon soil	Seward; A-hor. soil; 6th location on Quarry traverse	64.71754	-165.73883	<3
05AK061B	MRP-06121	C-257792	B-horizon soil	Seward; B-hor. soil; 6th location on Quarry traverse	64.71754	-165.73883	<3
05AK061C	MRP-06121	C-257793	C-horizon soil	Seward; C-hor. soil; 6th location on Quarry traverse	64.71754	-165.73883	<3
05AK071A	MRP-06121	C-257794	A-horizon soil	Seward; A-hor. soil; 7th location on Quarry traverse	64.72247	-165.73430	<3
05AK071B	MRP-06121	C-257795	B-horizon soil	Seward; B-hor. soil; 7th location on Quarry traverse	64.72247	-165.73430	<3
05AK071C	MRP-06121	C-257796	C-horizon soil	Seward; C-hor. soil; 7th location on Quarry traverse	64.72247	-165.73430	<3

Field no.	Al ICP-MS (%)	As ICP-MS (ppm)	Ba ICP-MS (ppm)	Be ICP-MS (ppm)	Bi ICP-MS (ppm)	Ca ICP-MS (ppm)	Cd ICP-MS (ppm)	Ce ICP-MS (ppm)	Co ICP-MS (ppm)	Cr ICP-MS (ppm)	Cs ICP-MS (ppm)	Cu ICP-MS (ppm)	F ISE (ppm)
05AK011A	8.43	27.0	1,710	2.78	0.240	4,020	4.58	80	13.4	96.5	14.9	28.8	1,480
05AK011B	8.96	32.8	1,910	3.07	0.248	2,810	5.86	88	17.0	96.2	15.6	37.0	1,700
05AK011C	9.25	47.3	2,050	3.38	0.253	3,490	6.58	94	17.0	109.0	16.6	27.9	1,950
05AK012A	6.50	36.7	2,700	2.44	0.249	9,120	8.63	45	15.0	62.2	9.1	22.6	1,440
05AK012B	7.46	41.4	4,300	2.73	0.235	5,420	3.84	71	11.7	63.8	9.5	23.3	1,870
05AK012C	7.72	52.3	4,900	2.94	0.260	4,610	4.86	76	19.5	66.4	9.9	31.4	2,040
05AK021A	6.83	28.6	936	3.05	0.210	18,800	3.91	56	13.9	61.7	8.0	21.8	1,760
05AK021B	7.47	36.6	946	3.32	0.218	7,320	3.74	85	14.0	67.4	9.1	20.5	1,880
05AK021C	6.67	39.8	832	2.96	0.195	5,550	3.62	92	13.1	61.3	9.9	18.9	1,490
05AK031A	5.12	21.0	467	1.86	0.210	18,300	1.61	54	13.2	58.2	4.2	22.7	661
05AK031B	6.25	25.8	562	2.32	0.237	13,700	1.33	76	15.9	71.6	5.8	26.1	809
05AK031C	6.70	29.2	594	2.37	0.248	9,580	1.33	92	18.3	78.4	6.0	27.7	828
05AK032A	3.38	10.8	307	1.25	0.130	28,700	1.19	34	8.5	37.2	2.2	19.0	520
05AK032B	5.66	17.8	518	2.20	0.197	19,600	1.17	54	13.5	65.7	5.7	25.6	845
05AK032C	5.56	24.4	484	2.04	0.195	15,700	1.18	81	17.2	59.6	4.5	24.6	851
05AK041A	3.09	10.4	349	1.21	0.166	28,700	1.23	37	7.3	29.9	2.9	16.7	471
05AK041B	6.44	14.7	798	2.56	0.236	29,400	0.97	106	12.4	61.6	8.7	24.0	930
05AK041C	7.75	14.7	1,110	2.92	0.256	32,800	0.98	99	14.5	73.3	11.5	21.6	1,000
05AK051A	6.32	14.0	528	2.12	0.277	21,800	0.51	57	9.9	51.0	4.8	18.4	644
05AK051B	7.97	11.6	572	2.03	0.172	23,000	0.32	63	8.3	26.2	2.6	13.6	466
05AK051C	6.68	22.9	600	2.49	0.229	69,600	0.57	81	14.2	62.6	4.3	19.8	624
05AK052A	6.72	19.1	611	2.07	0.263	12,700	0.46	64	14.2	75.6	5.3	27.9	660
05AK052B	8.07	21.0	695	2.64	0.270	10,100	0.20	78	16.8	82.5	6.0	26.7	702
05AK052C	7.94	23.5	708	2.60	0.256	9,340	0.18	101	19.5	80.5	5.9	28.2	750
05AK061A	7.78	10.0	704	2.86	0.243	11,600	0.13	94	12.6	71.9	8.8	30.6	1,230
05AK061B	8.48	9.0	780	3.06	0.216	14,300	0.07	129	13.8	75.6	9.6	18.1	1,350
05AK061C	8.05	9.4	685	3.05	0.149	20,500	0.09	97	12.3	67.8	8.5	18.1	1,280
05AK071A	2.92	18.0	287	1.49	0.149	94,900	0.55	43	6.2	32.0	0.9	16.0	412
05AK071B	2.66	20.7	256	1.23	0.113	223,000	0.20	37	5.8	28.2	0.2	13.7	232
05AK071C	2.62	16.7	247	1.24	0.111	244,000	0.19	39	6.4	27.2	0.1	14.9	260

Field no.	Fe ICP-MS (%)	Ga ICP-MS (ppm)	Hg CVAA (ppm)	K ICP-MS (%)	La ICP-MS (ppm)	Li ICP-MS (ppm)	Mg ICP-MS (ppm)	Mn ICP-MS (ppm)	Mo ICP-MS (ppm)	Na ICP-MS (ppm)	Nb ICP-MS (ppm)	Ni ICP-MS (ppm)	P ICP-MS (%)
05AK011A	3.44	19.3	0.23	3.68	37.2	46.0	7,140	476	0.47	3,710	5.2	32	0.063
05AK011B	4.92	20.1	0.36	3.92	40.3	46.7	7,200	671	0.38	3,640	4.1	38	0.061
05AK011C	5.86	20.2	0.26	4.12	43.2	48.1	6,850	1,240	0.76	3,430	2.8	49	0.110
05AK012A	4.14	14.6	0.52	2.28	21.1	33.5	5,550	1,100	1.28	3,810	4.2	21	0.120
05AK012B	4.21	16.9	1.10	2.48	32.8	41.4	6,610	566	0.67	5,360	6.5	24	0.085
05AK012C	4.98	17.3	1.05	2.61	33.8	42.5	6,740	1,120	0.69	5,380	7.3	25	0.079
05AK021A	4.31	14.8	0.14	2.82	28.0	32.9	7,220	1,580	0.50	2,980	3.5	42	0.106
05AK021B	4.41	16.5	0.09	3.25	39.6	36.6	7,400	678	0.36	3,120	4.4	45	0.071
05AK021C	4.86	16.0	0.09	2.64	37.4	30.2	6,200	1,160	0.50	2,820	5.3	45	0.061
05AK031A	4.10	12.5	0.07	1.30	26.1	25.1	6,690	1,540	0.60	4,920	6.6	26	0.117
05AK031B	5.07	15.0	0.06	1.59	32.8	29.5	7,910	1,630	0.62	5,770	8.7	31	0.114
05AK031C	5.56	16.1	0.06	1.63	35.4	31.7	8,370	1,700	0.54	6,460	9.6	34	0.106
05AK032A	2.56	8.0	0.09	0.92	17.3	16.3	5,340	834	0.47	3,210	3.2	17	0.113
05AK032B	4.28	13.7	0.07	1.58	27.9	27.8	8,330	1,160	0.60	4,890	6.4	27	0.125
05AK032C	4.90	13.4	0.05	1.42	32.4	25.4	8,110	1,500	0.46	6,480	5.4	28	0.088
05AK041A	2.92	7.8	0.11	1.11	18.5	11.8	4,270	1,370	0.49	2,430	<2	12	0.121
05AK041B	5.02	16.5	0.05	2.53	41.0	23.6	8,410	1,560	0.41	4,740	3.4	22	0.102
05AK041C	5.67	19.6	0.04	3.26	38.4	27.6	13,700	1,750	0.33	4,760	6.2	28	0.081
05AK051A	3.77	14.6	0.07	1.37	24.5	27.1	6,700	1,150	1.11	8,030	10.7	19	0.177
05AK051B	3.84	16.4	0.06	1.34	27.2	24.1	6,210	1,480	1.48	17,000	15.9	10	0.138
05AK051C	5.20	15.0	0.10	1.41	35.3	29.1	11,600	1,980	0.82	8,980	7.1	28	0.113
05AK052A	4.29	15.6	0.12	1.42	31.9	32.8	7,720	1,580	0.87	6,260	10.4	33	0.153
05AK052B	5.21	18.9	0.08	1.70	35.2	36.7	9,650	1,150	0.91	9,200	14.5	35	0.115
05AK052C	5.46	18.8	0.07	1.74	39.5	34.4	9,500	1,470	0.78	9,420	13.3	35	0.092
05AK061A	3.72	18.6	0.05	3.06	37.1	28.5	6,870	745	0.48	3,820	5.1	21	0.084
05AK061B	3.69	20.6	0.03	3.53	47.4	28.5	7,290	585	0.36	4,520	4.1	23	0.052
05AK061C	3.47	19.1	0.03	3.20	38.1	29.9	6,850	674	0.40	5,420	4.3	19	0.061
05AK071A	2.80	6.1	0.09	0.65	21.2	14.1	4,280	1,740	0.44	2,780	3.2	15	0.170
05AK071B	2.60	5.5	0.04	0.54	18.7	12.9	4,700	1,570	0.39	2,760	3.2	17	0.145
05AK071C	2.54	5.4	0.04	0.53	18.6	12.4	4,700	1,530	0.36	2,840	3.1	17	0.133

Field no.	Pb ICP-MS (ppm)	Rb ICP-MS (ppm)	Sb ICP-MS (ppm)	Sc ICP-MS (ppm)	Sr ICP-MS (ppm)	Th ICP-MS (ppm)	Ti ICP-MS (%)	Tl ICP-MS (ppm)	U ICP-MS (ppm)	V ICP-MS (ppm)	Y ICP-MS (ppm)	Zn ICP-MS (ppm)
05AK011A	594	188	9.5	17.1	54	14.3	0.230	1.410	1.53	118	24	1240
05AK011B	543	200	8.9	17.9	52	15.5	0.215	1.330	1.53	116	29	1630
05AK011C	394	208	8.0	18.0	52	15.7	0.190	1.380	1.53	117	32	1400
05AK012A	674	122	9.3	12.4	60	8.3	0.200	0.937	1.35	87	19	2710
05AK012B	768	126	12	13.6	68	11.3	0.273	1.020	1.75	97	28	3560
05AK012C	829	133	14	14.7	69	11.2	0.286	1.080	1.93	99	35	3890
05AK021A	72	142	5.2	12.0	82	9.0	0.184	1.150	1.40	81	34	930
05AK021B	79	151	5.9	12.7	57	12.8	0.214	1.240	1.54	90	38	656
05AK021C	87	127	7.2	11.8	48	10.3	0.168	1.130	1.31	74	35	701
05AK031A	38	72	3.1	12.3	128	7.6	0.275	0.597	1.49	93	28	204
05AK031B	48	85	3.9	15.2	125	9.1	0.339	0.724	1.66	114	35	221
05AK031C	52	85	3.9	16.0	118	10.0	0.373	0.757	1.84	126	37	221
05AK032A	18	50	2.0	8.6	134	4.6	0.168	0.389	1.17	62	20	139
05AK032B	29	82	3.4	14.3	131	8.1	0.294	0.646	1.56	105	31	184
05AK032C	39	72	4.0	14.5	126	9.6	0.387	0.595	1.59	106	33	184
05AK041A	18	54	1.8	7.2	74	5.0	0.101	0.434	1.26	44	19	247
05AK041B	17	130	2.1	14.4	96	12.7	0.170	0.761	1.31	84	34	306
05AK041C	15	170	2.0	16.7	91	11.8	0.197	0.918	1.37	95	36	347
05AK051A	15	68	3.9	13.2	156	7.5	0.340	0.629	2.57	83	27	161
05AK051B	13	51	2.1	15.4	197	6.8	0.475	0.447	2.44	69	40	122
05AK051C	17	74	4.2	14.7	270	8.7	0.346	0.640	1.92	100	36	175
05AK052A	16	78	3.6	15.3	119	8.5	0.356	0.743	1.89	114	31	150
05AK052B	19	89	3.6	17.6	141	10.0	0.494	0.763	2.11	140	30	129
05AK052C	20	92	3.8	18.0	142	11.3	0.539	0.771	2.06	139	32	113
05AK061A	17	148	2.6	15.7	78	11.7	0.176	0.882	1.74	84	31	71
05AK061B	15	166	1.8	15.8	90	14.7	0.166	0.926	1.58	87	27	61
05AK061C	16	149	1.9	14.9	115	11.9	0.176	0.867	1.57	80	31	59
05AK071A	8.9	33	4.9	7.9	260	3.8	0.129	0.399	0.97	50	31	75
05AK071B	9.3	28	4.0	7.1	568	3.3	0.134	0.310	0.96	46	29	48
05AK071C	7.3	27	3.8	7.0	614	3.5	0.128	0.291	0.94	44	30	48

Soil samples collected in the Solomon C-5 quadrangle (Big Hurrah) traverse

Field no.	Laboratory job no.	Laboratory no.	Sample description	Site description	Latitude	Longitude	Ag ICP-MS (ppm)
05AK081A	MRP-06125	C-257809	A-horizon soil	Seward; A-hor. soil; 1st location, 1st site on Big Hurrah traverse	64.66301	-164.29454	<3
05AK081B	MRP-06125	C-257810	B-horizon soil	Seward; B-hor. soil; 1st location, 1st site on Big Hurrah traverse	64.66301	-164.29454	<3
05AK081C	MRP-06125	C-257811	C-horizon soil	Seward; C-hor. soil; 1st location, 1st site on Big Hurrah traverse	64.66301	-164.29454	<3
05AK082A	MRP-06125	C-257812	A-horizon soil	Seward; A-hor. soil; 1st location, 2nd site on Big Hurrah traverse	64.66302	-164.29359	<3
05AK082B	MRP-06125	C-257813	B-horizon soil	Seward; B-hor. soil; 1st location, 2nd site on Big Hurrah traverse	64.66302	-164.29359	<3
05AK082C	MRP-06125	C-257814	C-horizon soil	Seward; C-hor. soil; 1st location, 2nd site on Big Hurrah traverse	64.66302	-164.29359	<3
05AK091A	MRP-06125	C-257815	A-horizon soil	Seward; A-hor. soil; 2nd location on Big Hurrah traverse	64.65839	-164.28967	<3
05AK091B	MRP-06125	C-257816	B-horizon soil	Seward; B-hor. soil; 2nd location on Big Hurrah traverse	64.65839	-164.28967	<3
05AK091C	MRP-06125	C-257817	C-horizon soil	Seward; C-hor. soil; 2nd location on Big Hurrah traverse	64.65839	-164.28967	<3
05AK101A	MRP-06125	C-257818	A-horizon soil	Seward; A-hor. soil; 3rd location, 1st site on Big Hurrah traverse	64.66301	-164.29454	<3
05AK101B	MRP-06125	C-257819	B-horizon soil	Seward; B-hor. soil; 3rd location, 1st site on Big Hurrah traverse	64.66301	-164.29454	<3
05AK101C	MRP-06125	C-257820	C-horizon soil	Seward; C-hor. soil; 3rd location, 1st site on Big Hurrah traverse	64.66301	-164.29454	<3
05AK102A	MRP-06125	C-257821	A-horizon soil	Seward; A-hor. soil; 3rd location, 2nd site on Big Hurrah traverse	64.65976	-164.27770	<3
05AK102B	MRP-06125	C-257822	B-horizon soil	Seward; B-hor. soil; 3rd location, 2nd site on Big Hurrah traverse	64.65976	-164.27770	<3
05AK102C	MRP-06125	C-257823	C-horizon soil	Seward; C-hor. soil; 3rd location, 2nd site on Big Hurrah traverse	64.65976	-164.27770	<3
05AK111A	MRP-06125	C-257823	A-horizon soil	Seward; A-hor. soil; 4th location, 1st site on Big Hurrah traverse	64.66183	-164.27782	<3
05AK111B	MRP-06125	C-257823	B-horizon soil	Seward; B-hor. soil; 4th location, 1st site on Big Hurrah traverse	64.66183	-164.27782	<3
05AK111C	MRP-06125	C-257823	C-horizon soil	Seward; C-hor. soil; 4th location, 1st site on Big Hurrah traverse	64.66183	-164.27782	<3
05AK121A	MRP-06125	C-257824	A-horizon soil	Seward; A-hor. soil; 4th location, 2nd site on Big Hurrah traverse	64.66342	-164.27788	<3
05AK121B	MRP-06125	C-257825	B-horizon soil	Seward; B-hor. soil; 4th location, 2nd site on Big Hurrah traverse	64.66342	-164.27788	<3
05AK121C	MRP-06125	C-257826	C-horizon soil	Seward; C-hor. soil; 4th location, 2nd site on Big Hurrah traverse	64.66342	-164.27788	<3
05AK131A	MRP-06125	C-257827	A-horizon soil	Seward; A-hor. soil; 5th location, 1st site on Big Hurrah traverse	64.66610	-164.28725	<3
05AK131B	MRP-06125	C-257828	B-horizon soil	Seward; B-hor. soil; 5th location, 1st site on Big Hurrah traverse	64.66610	-164.28725	<3
05AK131C	MRP-06125	C-257829	C-horizon soil	Seward; C-hor. soil; 5th location, 1st site on Big Hurrah traverse	64.66610	-164.28725	<3
05AK132A	MRP-06125	C-257830	A-horizon soil	Seward; A-hor. soil; 5th location, 2nd site on Big Hurrah traverse	64.66584	-164.28813	<3
05AK132B	MRP-06125	C-257831	B-horizon soil	Seward; B-hor. soil; 5th location, 2nd site on Big Hurrah traverse	64.66584	-164.28813	<3
05AK132C	MRP-06125	C-257832	C-horizon soil	Seward; C-hor. soil; 5th location, 2nd site on Big Hurrah traverse	64.66584	-164.28813	<3
05AK141A	MRP-06125	C-257833	A-horizon soil	Seward; A-hor. soil; 6th location on Big Hurrah traverse	64.66360	-164.28433	<3
05AK141B	MRP-06125	C-257834	B-horizon soil	Seward; B-hor. soil; 6th location on Big Hurrah traverse	64.66360	-164.28433	<3
05AK141C	MRP-06125	C-257835	C-horizon soil	Seward; C-hor. soil; 6th location on Big Hurrah traverse	64.66360	-164.28433	<3
05AK151A	MRP-06125	C-257836	A-horizon soil	Seward; A-hor. soil; 7th location on Big Hurrah traverse	64.66396	-164.27846	<3
05AK151B	MRP-06125	C-257837	B-horizon soil	Seward; B-hor. soil; 7th location on Big Hurrah traverse	64.66396	-164.27846	<3
05AK151C	MRP-06125	C-257838	C-horizon soil	Seward; C-hor. soil; 7th location on Big Hurrah traverse	64.66396	-164.27846	<3

Field no.	Al ICP-MS (%)	As ICP-MS (ppm)	Ba ICP-MS (ppm)	Be ICP-MS (ppm)	Bi ICP-MS (ppm)	Ca ICP-MS (ppm)	Cd ICP-MS (ppm)	Ce ICP-MS (ppm)	Co ICP-MS (ppm)	Cr ICP-MS (ppm)	Cs ICP-MS (ppm)	Cu ICP-MS (ppm)	F ISE (ppm)
05AK081A	8.43	31.9	2,830	2.67	0.262	1,630	0.75	42	8.4	122.0	6.2	57.0	726
05AK081B	9.20	35.2	3,050	2.88	0.300	1,170	0.60	62	9.7	133.0	7.2	72.9	770
05AK081C	8.35	42.9	2,850	2.68	0.264	784	0.87	56	14.8	122.0	5.8	66.8	735
05AK082A	4.97	30.1	1,920	1.61	0.230	3,690	2.37	35	4.9	61.4	3.9	32.8	416
05AK082B	7.83	28.8	2,120	2.10	0.258	3,250	0.48	40	4.7	100.0	5.6	49.5	529
05AK082C	7.59	33.8	2,260	2.07	0.263	3,060	0.52	41	7.8	114.0	5.5	55.7	609
05AK091A	2.69	23.5	2,420	1.10	0.113	1,350	2.50	21	6.1	58.7	0.2	38.8	382
05AK091B	4.66	51.4	4,590	1.96	0.205	1,460	1.46	38	11.1	115.0	2.1	89.0	662
05AK091C	5.69	48.8	5,020	2.12	0.241	2,060	2.03	88	13.3	135.0	3.4	142.0	727
05AK101A	4.41	53.7	2,010	1.41	0.207	2,030	1.74	32	6.0	74.9	2.6	40.2	459
05AK101B	5.90	70.7	2,710	1.87	0.256	2,090	1.11	42	8.4	102.0	3.6	56.0	547
05AK101C	5.04	71.2	2,590	1.95	0.213	1,550	1.36	42	10.9	94.4	2.5	57.2	529
05AK102A	4.30	71.7	2,910	1.63	0.242	638	1.46	35	5.8	97.4	2.9	65.1	563
05AK102B	4.68	112.0	3,590	1.89	0.329	462	2.23	38	11.3	124.0	3.9	113.0	645
05AK102C	5.26	126.0	4,020	2.32	0.310	709	3.25	56	17.7	139.0	4.5	140.0	720
05AK111A	5.04	168.0	2,570	2.16	0.334	1,240	2.16	39	8.1	137.0	2.6	105.0	510
05AK111B	4.54	105.0	2,810	2.12	0.213	1,440	1.88	34	10.3	104.0	1.5	76.2	543
05AK111C	4.76	110.0	2,840	2.19	0.209	1,310	1.94	35	11.4	111.0	1.4	79.3	617
05AK121A	2.81	202.0	1,230	1.03	0.145	1,250	0.80	20	9.0	52.1	< 0.003	29.5	399
05AK121B	5.77	681.0	1,500	1.90	0.255	1,410	0.60	45	21.7	106.0	0.2	57.8	536
05AK121C	5.96	612.0	1,520	2.04	0.265	1,490	0.53	49	20.9	107.0	0.5	57.4	594
05AK131A	5.43	210.0	2,460	1.81	0.292	1,270	1.05	40	8.6	96.3	3.5	72.0	463
05AK131B	6.11	211.0	2,530	1.99	0.266	1,450	1.03	39	10.1	102.0	3.8	74.8	515
05AK131C	5.42	196.0	2,570	1.87	0.241	1,110	1.07	38	10.1	88.5	3.0	125.0	500
05AK132A	6.36	156.0	2,450	2.27	0.190	1,320	3.86	50	22.8	167.0	3.5	82.5	522
05AK132B	6.13	166.0	2,700	2.27	0.210	1,400	3.88	44	19.1	125.0	4.1	78.0	535
05AK132C	6.65	227.0	2,780	2.37	0.229	1,150	3.88	45	19.7	131.0	4.3	82.2	636
05AK141A	3.03	34.3	3,060	1.26	0.121	750	0.32	23	2.2	48.5	1.8	24.0	434
05AK141B	2.79	38.4	3,250	1.37	0.118	356	0.20	20	1.8	43.0	1.0	24.6	339
05AK141C	3.05	43.0	3,500	1.40	0.114	273	0.24	19	2.5	47.0	1.1	35.0	345
05AK151A	6.50	168.0	1,910	2.39	0.350	3,740	1.14	69	35.4	128.0	1.3	63.0	892
05AK151B	6.80	115.0	1,890	2.76	0.387	3,310	1.23	69	42.4	129.0	1.3	67.6	899
05AK151C	6.67	111.0	1,940	2.60	0.362	3,460	1.55	73	36.2	136.0	1.5	66.1	904

41

Field no.	Fe ICP-MS (%)	Ga ICP-MS (ppm)	Hg CVAA (ppm)	K ICP-MS (%)	La ICP-MS (ppm)	Li ICP-MS (ppm)	Mg ICP-MS (ppm)	Mn ICP-MS (ppm)	Mo ICP-MS (ppm)	Na ICP-MS (ppm)	Nb ICP-MS (ppm)	Ni ICP-MS (ppm)	P ICP-MS (%)
05AK081A	4.70	18.4	0.07	2.37	19.6	40.2	9,170	213	21.50	7,210	4.6	56	0.093
05AK081B	4.81	20.0	0.06	2.54	27.2	45.8	10,300	217	23.50	7,380	5.1	65	0.099
05AK081C	5.04	18.4	0.05	2.32	25.9	42.5	9,590	397	24.20	7,210	5.8	69	0.091
05AK082A	2.58	12.0	0.17	1.15	16.4	27.6	5,700	209	16.80	4,840	4.5	25	0.117
05AK082B	3.86	17.3	0.09	1.83	18.2	34.1	8,550	260	23.10	10,000	7.4	24	0.107
05AK082C	4.99	18.3	0.05	2.00	20.8	33.0	8,950	301	30.20	10,600	7.1	34	0.106
05AK091A	2.20	6.8	0.14	0.80	10.3	11.9	3,760	176	8.76	1,930	4.0	35	0.117
05AK091B	4.72	11.4	0.12	1.37	18.5	22.5	6,330	296	15.60	2,500	5.2	65	0.136
05AK091C	4.66	13.6	0.16	1.56	35.5	28.7	8,050	280	17.00	3,550	6.7	82	0.145
05AK101A	3.46	12.0	0.09	0.99	15.1	29.2	4,460	226	11.60	4,050	6.8	33	0.138
05AK101B	4.73	14.8	0.08	1.24	22.6	39.1	5,850	341	13.40	4,440	8.9	44	0.118
05AK101C	4.56	12.6	0.05	1.12	22.2	36.9	5,280	408	11.60	3,370	6.5	49	0.112
05AK102A	3.09	11.3	0.07	1.13	17.3	20.5	4,180	133	14.10	2,170	4.1	41	0.111
05AK102B	5.04	11.9	0.06	1.33	21.2	23.8	4,480	231	15.50	1,690	5.1	73	0.109
05AK102C	5.71	12.4	0.08	1.49	26.9	28.9	4,930	447	14.50	1,680	6.1	92	0.123
05AK111A	6.39	12.3	0.07	1.21	19.0	37.6	6,500	188	22.40	3,460	4.8	57	0.177
05AK111B	5.42	11.0	0.05	1.20	16.5	28.3	6,990	282	15.10	2,510	4.7	62	0.150
05AK111C	5.59	11.1	0.05	1.26	16.7	30.1	7,980	347	13.80	2,760	5.1	56	0.145
05AK121A	3.21	7.2	0.14	0.60	9.2	19.7	7,030	413	7.16	2,480	2.0	37	0.123
05AK121B	7.94	13.1	0.04	0.89	20.6	43.8	17,700	958	7.61	4,540	3.6	78	0.136
05AK121C	7.88	13.7	0.03	0.95	22.2	43.7	17,300	939	7.58	5,180	4.4	74	0.127
05AK131A	4.83	14.4	0.05	1.28	19.1	39.0	5,290	308	13.80	3,860	7.0	59	0.111
05AK131B	5.14	15.1	0.08	1.33	21.2	43.9	5,860	357	13.30	4,240	7.8	63	0.100
05AK131C	4.99	13.2	0.07	1.17	17.9	38.5	5,140	308	17.80	3,290	7.0	84	0.088
05AK132A	4.62	14.8	0.05	1.42	24.2	47.3	13,600	815	12.50	4,090	6.1	150	0.072
05AK132B	4.32	14.9	0.03	1.52	22.2	46.8	9,470	867	14.00	3,720	6.6	121	0.077
05AK132C	4.71	15.7	0.06	1.67	22.6	48.7	10,500	900	14.50	4,050	7.2	123	0.074
05AK141A	1.11	8.6	0.08	0.84	11.6	17.8	2,900	64.8	14.50	1,830	3.9	26	0.049
05AK141B	1.17	8.1	0.02	0.78	10.6	18.6	2,660	55.9	14.70	1,240	3.1	27	0.028
05AK141C	1.34	8.2	0.03	0.83	9.6	21.3	2,900	65	16.50	947	2.8	33	0.029
05AK151A	10.10	14.3	0.03	1.22	29.1	33.4	21,200	1,160	3.94	6,760	7.4	99	0.211
05AK151B	10.90	15.1	0.02	1.36	28.6	35.6	23,200	1,350	5.37	7,050	5.6	127	0.197
05AK151C	11.10	15.0	0.03	1.34	30.1	35.5	21,800	1,310	5.43	6,310	6.6	116	0.230

Field no.	Pb ICP-MS (ppm)	Rb ICP-MS (ppm)	Sb ICP-MS (ppm)	Sc ICP-MS (ppm)	Sr ICP-MS (ppm)	Th ICP-MS (ppm)	Ti ICP-MS (%)	Ti ICP-MS (ppm)	U ICP-MS (ppm)	V ICP-MS (ppm)	Y ICP-MS (ppm)	Zn ICP-MS (ppm)
05AK081A	21	110	12	18.3	77	6.9	0.198	1.260	10.60	352	11	169
05AK081B	25	120	14	20.8	82	9.3	0.215	1.360	14.60	378	16	187
05AK081C	22	108	18	18.8	80	9.3	0.217	1.370	12.20	374	14	195
05AK082A	18	65	11	10.3	72	4.5	0.177	1.200	5.56	246	14	94
05AK082B	22	82	11	18.5	80	5.8	0.283	1.110	12.40	340	17	100
05AK082C	24	103	13	19.4	88	7.1	0.269	1.110	11.20	374	14	124
05AK091A	10	41	7.5	6.0	28	2.6	0.139	0.949	2.84	241	6.5	128
05AK091B	19	71	16	9.6	42	5.2	0.196	1.640	5.02	450	12	263
05AK091C	23	85	19	12.9	59	8.6	0.236	1.810	7.49	483	23	336
05AK101A	14	61	15	9.0	56	4.7	0.214	1.100	3.43	289	11	120
05AK101B	18	75	21	11.6	68	6.4	0.284	1.390	4.21	394	13	178
05AK101C	17	66	21	10.0	58	6.7	0.209	1.360	4.06	380	11	175
05AK102A	16	64	35	8.9	47	5.1	0.161	1.580	4.64	374	8.6	217
05AK102B	24	75	70	9.6	51	6.0	0.191	1.820	5.31	453	11	412
05AK102C	28	82	78	10.9	61	7.4	0.229	1.890	6.58	472	15	493
05AK111A	38	75	29	10.5	128	5.4	0.169	2.180	8.10	485	16	217
05AK111B	21	67	22	9.2	72	5.1	0.169	1.930	6.97	399	11	200
05AK111C	22	68	22	9.6	71	5.1	0.190	2.010	6.27	401	11	201
05AK121A	7.8	36	11	6.2	31	2.9	0.097	0.709	2.48	192	4.9	96
05AK121B	14	52	21	11.6	51	6.6	0.151	0.949	3.96	324	12	161
05AK121C	16	54	20	12.4	57	7.1	0.172	0.998	4.41	332	14	167
05AK131A	18	84	26	10.9	64	5.8	0.236	1.470	5.76	369	8.1	200
05AK131B	19	85	25	11.8	69	6.8	0.266	1.490	6.68	382	9.2	209
05AK131C	17	73	27	10.9	63	6.5	0.234	1.380	9.81	381	9.1	244
05AK132A	13	80	16	15.6	59	7.4	0.282	1.350	9.67	331	17	281
05AK132B	15	86	19	14.4	65	7.6	0.254	1.500	9.05	359	15	288
05AK132C	16	94	19	15.7	63	7.9	0.277	1.550	10.30	358	16	263
05AK141A	6.5	48	16	6.4	37	3.1	0.152	1.300	3.38	348	5.6	86
05AK141B	6.1	45	20	5.6	32	2.8	0.140	1.270	3.31	391	5.0	77
05AK141C	7.6	46	25	6.0	36	3.1	0.136	1.320	4.48	410	6.3	97
05AK151A	18	67	6.5	13.8	73	8.6	0.266	1.160	4.91	310	22	152
05AK151B	20	72	6.7	14.7	75	8.9	0.232	1.240	5.46	318	23	166
05AK151C	20	73	6.5	14.8	75	8.7	0.238	1.250	5.51	321	25	174